FOR ADDITIONAL COPIES CALL
1-800-227-2309 EXT
59147
$6.95

KT-369-182

# Divided by a Common Language

A British / American dictionary PLUS

by

Christopher Davies

Published by Mayflower Press
Sarasota, Florida

# Divided by a Common Language

## A British / American dictionary PLUS

### by Christopher Davies

Cover design by Shawn Peters

Illustrated by Jason Murphy

Printed by Rose Printing Co., Inc.

Published by Mayflower Press

MayflowerP@aol.com

Copyright © 1997 by Christopher Davies  All rights reserved.  No part of this book may be reproduced or transmitted in any form without written permission from the author, except for brief quotations in a review.

ISBN  0-9660945-7-3

Library of Congress Catalog Card Number 97-94724

# TABLE OF CONTENTS

George Bernard Shaw once said "England and America are two countries divided by a common language."

# FOREWORD

Since my first trip to the United States in 1979, I have been struck by the magnitude of the differences between British and American speech. Some experts estimate that there are roughly 4,000 words in everyday speech that are used differently. One might assume that Australia and New Zealand, for example, might have equally big differences in language and culture from their Mother Country, but not so. I found the differences in these two countries to be quite superficial in comparison with those of the United States. Of course slang expressions are quite different, but spelling and word usage are much the same. In fact recently, with Australian television shows being broadcast in Britain, some Australian slang is finding its way back home. By contrast, Canada, with its major cities all within a few hours drive of the U.S. border, has only a vestige of its British speech remaining in the English speaking sections, (though it still uses mostly British spelling) and to most outsiders appears thoroughly American. The aim of this book is to give Americans and Britons a better understanding of each other's variation of the English language.

# ACKNOWLEDGEMENTS

The author gratefully acknowledges the help and advice received from the Smithsonian Institute in Washington, DC, and from family and the many friends and acquaintances whose patience made this book possible.

*"How about a short stack with some links John...?"*

(see page 24)

*Noah Webster, the well known American lexicographer, forecast back in 1789 that eventually American English would be as different from British English as Dutch, Danish and Swedish are from German, or from each another*

# WHAT HAPPENED TO ENGLISH IN AMERICA ?

*A* British reader looking at a newspaper or magazine from Australia or South Africa would not find too many unfamiliar words. Not so with American English. Words such as:

- caboose, bleachers and busboy

which are everyday words in America, would perplex the average speaker of British English. Here are some words used in British English, that an American might find a little strange:

- mailshot, crosspatch and gymkhana

(These words can all be found in the lexicon.)

Most English speaking people are unaware of the vast differences between British and American English. This book is designed to enlighten the reader about these differences, and briefly explain how these differences came about.

## SOME ANSWERS

Why, when we have global communication on the Internet and we are all watching the same television shows do we still have difficulty understanding one another? An estimated 4,000 words in everyday use in Britain, have a different meaning or are used differently in the U.S. Let's go back in time to find some answers.

The early settlers in the U.S. had no verbal contact with the folk they left behind in England, and the division of the language began. Over the years many Europeans settled in the U.S., bringing their languages with them. English remained the dominant language in America, though German was widely spoken in the 1800's. There were numerous French colonies, and New York was originally a Dutch settlement, called New Amsterdam. Each language left its mark on spoken English, with mainly the written word standardizing speech. Until the 1900's many books were imported from England, which did keep American English from straying too far.

Noah Webster, the well known American lexicographer, forecast back in 1789 that eventually American English would be as different from British English, as Dutch, Danish and Swedish are from German, or from each another. This may sound preposterous, but Webster himself did initiate some of the biggest changes in American spelling and pronunciation. His *American Dictionary of the English Language* became the standard for spelling and word usage in America.

British and American English probably reached their greatest divergence just before the second world war and since that time have been getting closer, or at least better understood, by the other country.

It is odd that although Webster initiated a lot of changes in American English, some expressions that Americans use today have died out in Britain.

Here are some expressions currently used in the U.S., which were once well known in Britain, but have long since gone out of use there.

- Son of a gun

- I guess

- In back of (for behind)

A word that is no longer used in Britain but is still in current use in America is *gotten* for the past participle of the verb *to get*. It is only used in British English with the expression *Ill gotten gains*. To the American ear, the sentence *It has got to the point where...*, sounds grammatically incorrect. They would say, *It has gotten to the point where...*.

Some other words that have died out in Britain, but are still used in America are: *Turnpike,* (for toll road), *Fall* (for autumn), and a *Deck of cards* (for a pack of cards.) Conversely the word *straight away* meaning immediately and *presently* meaning in a short time are no longer in common usage in America, but are often used in British English.

## THE INDUSTRIAL REVOLUTION

Then along came the industrial revolution, bringing with it a need for many new words such as:

- railroad, windshield and grade crossing.

America was no longer conforming to the British standard with new words. Britain was already using the words:

- railway, windscreen and level crossing

Each country had its own engineers and designers, who gave new creations their particular names. Hundreds of new terms were needed. Of course these words were scarcely in print at the time, so there was no written standard to follow. With the countries so far apart there was really no need for the U.S. to follow the British terms. The differences increased as time went on, even though more people were traveling back and forth across the Atlantic by now. Many educated people were aware of the differences in terminology, but no great effort was made to unify the terms. The differences between British and American English gradually increased, until greater communication between the countries in the 1940's turned the tide. A good example of how far apart the languages had become, is apparent in the list of railway terms. (See p.64)

Despite all of the communication going on between Britain and America today, it is amazing that new words being coined in one country are represented by another word in the other country.

*Some examples of relatively new American words:*

- pound for the # symbol
- popsicle (in the U.K., an ice lolly)
- dumpster (in the U.K., a skip)

*Some newer British words that might not be understood by the average American are:*

- video (in the U.S., a V.C.R.)
- flex (in the U.S., electrical cord)
- bumf (in the U.S., unwanted papers and documents)

The United States is a huge country and has a diversity of slang and accents much as Britain does. When one considers its size, it has a surprisingly uniform speech pattern, in large because of the media and the mobility of the population. One major difference between the U.K. and the U.S. is the fact that while in Britain people from different levels of society speak with very different accents, there is little variation in accent among different classes of Americans, (though this is not always true in big cities.)

## THE IMPACT OF IMMIGRATION

In order to understand why British English is so different from American English, it is necessary to learn something about the settlement of the United States. For many settlers in America, English was not their native tongue. Broken English was commonplace when immigration was at its peak. Many foreigners would mispronounce words and those who learned English from books were prone to speaking words as they thought they should be pronounced. Noah Webster in his best selling *American Speller*, published in 1783, suggested giving every letter in a syllable its due proportion of sound. This in part explains why Americans tend to pronounce word endings more fully than the British. In particular, words ending with; ARY, ORY and ERY, in which the vowel becomes lost when pronounced in British English.

## COUNTRIES WHICH ENRICHED THE AMERICAN LANGUAGE

### France

Two hundred years ago, French was rivaling English for the number one international language. There were many French colonies in the U.S. The largest and also the most influential on the language, was in the Mississippi delta. The state Louisiana gets its name from Louis XIV. The Cajuns came to Louisiana from Arcadia, Nova Scotia. (Somewhere along the way Arcadians became known as Cajuns.) Here are some words the French settlers gave the English language: *Bayou* (for a marshy inlet), *Gopher* (for a ground squirrel), and *Levee*, (for a dike).

*Pronouncing French place names:*

| | |
|---|---|
| Versailles, in Kentucky: | ver·**sales** |
| Des Moines, in Iowa: | duh·**moyn** |
| St Louis, in Missouri: | saint lewis |
| Pierre, in South Dakota: | peer |
| Terre Haute, in Indiana | terra **hote** |

## The Netherlands

The Dutch had a large colony in what is now known as New York (originally New Amsterdam) by the mid 1600's. Brooklyn, Harlem and The Bronx are all derived from Dutch names. The Dutch left a legacy of the following words:

- caboose, coleslaw, cookie, and waffle.

## Spain

The Spanish conquistadors left a hefty legacy of place names behind. In addition, they left Americans many words which are associated with cowboys these days, such as: *Lasso, mustang, rodeo,* and *burro.* The constant influx of Hispanics from south of the border is creating what is called *Spanglish* in certain parts of the U.S.

*Some words of Spanish origin that are everyday words in American English:*

- coyote (a wild wolflike dog)    pronounced kie·oh·tee
- adobe (a clay and straw brick)    pronounced a·**doh**·bee
- mesa (a high piece of land)    pronounced **may**·sa

*Pronouncing Spanish place names:*

| | |
|---|---|
| La Jolla, in California | la hoya |
| El Cajon, in California | el ca·**hone** |
| St Augustine in Florida | saint **aug**·usteen |
| El Paso, in Texas | el passo |

## Germany

About seven million Germans have settled in the U.S. Not wishing to forget their country of origin, they have named twelve towns Berlin and seven towns Germantown. Here are some words the Germans added to American English.

- bummer, check (in a restaurant), docent, nix

## Central European Countries

Many Jews from Central Europe settled in New York. Yiddish expressions are widely used in America, but New York still leads the field in the use of these adulterated German words. Here are some examples:

- chutzpah      impudence / nerve
- kibitz, to      give unsolicited advice / joke around
- kosher      genuine / legitimate
- klutz      clumsy person
- schlep, to      trudge / lug
- schmaltz      exaggerated sentimentalism
- schmooze      chat / gossip
- schnoz      a large nose
- tush      backside

## PRONOUNCING BRITISH PLACE NAMES

There are some cities and towns in England that are not pronounced phonetically.  Here are a few examples:

- Birmingham     **bir**·ming·um
- Beaulieu     beeoo·lee
- Bicester     bis·ter
- Derby     dar·bee
- Greenwich     gren·ich
- Leicester     les·ter
- Norwich     norr·ich
- Warwick     worr·ik
- Thames     tems  (a river)

*Written English in Australia, New Zealand and South Africa is very much closer to British English than American English*

# TIPS FOR THE TOURIST

## AT THE AIRPORT

There are some different terms which you will encounter as soon as you step of the airplane (or aeroplane as the British say.)

*Here are some terms heard at airports that often cause confusion:*

- A *skycap* in the U.S. is an airport porter

- One *hires* a car in the U.K., rents in the U.S.

- It's a taxi *rank* in the U.K., rather than taxi stand

## AT THE HOTEL

In the U.S., the ground floor of any building is known as the first floor. What is known in Britain as the first floor is called the second floor in the U.S.; the second, the third floor etc. An *efficiency* in the U.S. is a room with a small kitchen as well as a bathroom. The British hotel term *en-suite*, meaning with a bathroom, is not understood in the U.S. Duvets, which are found everywhere in Britain are not at all common in the U.S. In a British hotel or bed and breakfast establishment, you may be offered *half board*. This is similar to the U.S. term *American plan* i.e. breakfast and dinner are included in the price. Motels are not common in England. Many more moderately priced British hotels will have rooms with a shared bathroom, and often no television or telephone in the room. They have a lounge with a television, and often a dining room. Curiously the word accommodation is never used in the plural in British English. In the U.S. you make arrangements for *accommodations*.

*Here are some British hotel terms that can cause confusion:*

- reception means front desk
- a receptionist is a desk clerk
- a flannel is a washcloth
- a cot means a crib
- a communicating door is a connecting door.
- a tariff means a rate

In Britain a *faucet* is called a tap, a *full size bed* is known only as a double bed, a *twin size bed* is called a single bed, and a *rollaway* bed is known as a *fold up bed.*

# *PRACTICAL INFORMATION*

## THE BRITISH AUTOMOBILE

British rental cars do not usually come with automatic transmission unless you specifically request it. They are small by American standards and rarely have air conditioning. All British cars have repeater signals on the side of the car, which come on when you signal that you are turning. This enables cars alongside you to be aware of your intentions. Controls on British cars are generally similar to American cars these days, but of course one drives a car sitting on the right. British cars come with a hand brake for parking.

## THE AMERICAN AUTOMOBILE

All rental cars in the U.S. have automatic transmission and air conditioning as standard equipment, and all but the smallest, known as *sub compacts*, will have power steering and power brakes. Manual transmission is usually available upon request. Compact cars are probably as big as the average British car. Mid size and full size cars will seem quite roomy.

Don't be surprised if your car has automatic seat belts. When you shut your door, the shoulder restraint part of the belt will whirr across a track just above your window and hold you snugly in place. Don't forget to fasten the lap portion of the belt. Wearing a seat belt in the front seats is required by law in most States. You may not be able to shift out of park without first putting your foot on the brake pedal. You will not find a hand brake in larger cars. These will be equipped with a parking brake pedal, located at the upper far left of the driver's left leg. Once engaged, the parking brake will remain set until it is released manually, usually by pulling the lever marked "brake release" located under the dashboard just above the parking brake pedal. In some newer model cars, the parking brake is automatically released when you shift out of park. The parking brake pedal is equivalent to a hand brake, which is found in some smaller cars. Americans often refer to this brake is as the *emergency brake*. The automatic transmission selector or *gear shift* is usually situated on the column. If this is the case, the key cannot be removed unless the selector is in park. With a floor mounted selector there may be a small button located near the key which must be depressed in order to remove the key.

## GASOLINE (PETROL)

There are three grades of petrol (gasoline) commonly available in Britain today; four star, which contains lead, is 97 octane, premium unleaded is about 95 octane and super unleaded is about 98 octane. Premium unleaded, despite its name, has the lowest octane commonly available in Britain, but has a high enough octane for most modern cars. Petrol is sold by the litre (liter).

All gas in the U.S. is unleaded. It comes in three grades: regular, which is 87 octane; a mid grade of 89 octane, also known as unleaded plus; and premium or super, which may be as high as 94 octane, depending on the brand. Petrol is still sold by the gallon in the U.S. and is incredibly cheap by European standards. The U.S. gallon is based on a sixteen ounce pint, rather than the British twenty ounce pint, and therefore is smaller. A U.S. gallon is just under four liters. Americans sometimes use the colloquial expression *to gas up* a vehicle. Payment can often be made with a credit card at the pump.

## TELEPHONES

### British Telephones

Public telephones in Britain are mainly operated by British Telecom. Local calls are not unlimited for a flat rate as they often are in the U.S. British payphones will accept a variety of coins and even the most expensive call may be initiated with a 10 p. coin. Many people use a B.T. phone card at British payphones. These can be purchased at shops and post offices in varying denominations. They are inserted into a slot on the phone and a display tells you how much value remains on the card. The card is thrown away when its value is zero. If you have a telephone account with British Telecom, you can obtain a BT *charge card,* which enables you to bill a call to your account from any telephone. Long distance calls in Britain always start with the number 0. Local calls from a private home or business are charged by the minute. (This naturally cuts down on telephone solicitation.) A toll free long distance number is known as a Freefone or Freephone number. They usually start 0-800 or 0-500. The British phones ring with a distinctive double ring. An area code is also known as an S.T.D. code. (Subscriber Trunk Dialling.)

### American Telephones

A local call from a U.S. pay phone is on average twenty-five cents. Usually you pick up the hand set, put in the money, then dial the number. Some independently owned pay phones require you to dial the number first, then deposit the money. Although some of the independent companies do have time limit, there is usually no time limit on local calls,. The ringing tone is distinctive, because American phones do not ring with a double ring as do the British phones.

Local calls from a private phone are often free. Long distance calls always start with a 1. Just because a number happens to be in the same area code as the one you are calling from, doesn't mean that it is a local call. You may well have to dial 1 followed by the same area code and then the number you want, in order to reach that number. A recording will tell you if it is necessary to do this. To make a long distance call from a pay phone using coins, dial 1, then the area code, followed by the number. You will then hear a recording instructing you on how much money to deposit for a three minute conversation.

There are no nationally available phone cards like those in the United Kingdom; but in some locations and at all airports, you will find phones that do accept credit cards and personal phone cards known as *calling cards*. Phone cards of independent phone companies may be purchased at various shops. These, however, require you first to dial the company's toll free number found on the phone card, then your account number, prior to your dialing the number you want. Credits are deducted from the card until it expires. These cards have only been available since 1991.

Many businesses have *toll free* numbers which require dialing 1-800 or 1-888 before the exchange number. These toll free numbers, popularly known as eight-hundred numbers, are more common in America than in Britain. If you have a private telephone in the U.S., you can order a *calling card*, which is the equivalent of the BT *charge card*. This makes long distance phoning from a pay phone much easier. Beware of the letter O. It is not the same key as the number 0 in the U.S. Ph. Is sometimes used as an abbreviation for telephone as well as Tel.

*Some U.S. to U.K. phone term comparisons:*

- The symbol #, known as pound in the U.S. is called hash or square in the U.K.

- Caller ID in the U.S is known as caller display in the U.K.

- Call forwarding is known as call diversion

- A calling card is the equivalent of the BT charge card

- A busy signal is known as an engaged signal

- An unlisted number is known as an ex-directory number

- Information or directory assistance is known as directory inquiries

# FOR THE TECHNICALLY MINDED

## PLUMBING

*T*he plumbing system in Britain differs slightly from that in the U.S. In Britain the word tap is used for indoor and outdoor plumbing In the U.S. indoor taps are known as *faucets*, and outdoor taps are known as *spigots*. The term tap water is used in both countries however. In the U.S. the cold faucet is uniformly on the right for safety reasons. This is not true in Britain, where it can be found on either side. Household hot water systems differ. In Britain, the hot water tank is usually fed from a tank in the attic (known as a *cistern*), so that an overheated tank cannot blow back into the main supply line. In the U.S. hot water tanks are fed directly from the water supply to the house (known as the *mains* in Britain.) Thus the hot and cold water are at the same pressure, making mixer taps almost standard and very convenient.

Toilets in the U.S., though similar in appearance, have major differences. The equipment in the tank (known as a cistern in Britain) is very simple: a float and stop valve for maintaining the water level in the tank; and a rubber seal, known as a flapper, which sits over the outlet pipe at the bottom of the tank. The flapper is connected by a chain to the handle. When the handle is pushed down, it pulls up the chain, in turn raising the flapper and releasing the water. The system works admirably, but as the flapper ages it does not always maintain a good seal, resulting in a waste of water. For this reason, this system is not permitted in Britain, where a diaphragm is used to start a siphon effect from the tank into the bowl. In the U.S. the toilet bowls are all of the siphonic type. As the tank empties into the bowl , a siphon effect forms in the "S" bend in the base of the toilet, resulting in a rapid emptying of the bowl, followed by a gurgle. This system gives a good flush and is reasonably quiet but tends to block up more readily than the standard British system that relies solely on a rush of water.

## ELECTRICITY

In the U.S., electricity at the electrical outlet is 120 volts AC, 60 hertz. Plugs are mostly two pin, or three pin if they have an *ground* pin. Outlets are usually paired, one above the other. There are two vertical slots with a hole below for the ground. Older two slot outlets with no ground are still found in older buildings. Appliances are fitted with a molded plug. With high wattage appliances, it is normal for the plug to get warm! Most kitchen appliances have only two flat pins; but to make them safer, one pin is slightly wider than the other. The outlet also has different slot sizes so the plug can only be inserted right way up. These plugs are called *polarized* plugs. This way the appliance gets current only as far as its switch, until it is turned on. Refrigerators and microwave ovens, however, are all fitted with a ground pin. Light bulbs have a screw fitting rather than the British bayonet fitting, though the bayonet type is used in cars. Some light bulbs have two filaments giving a possibility of three levels of brightness. These are known as three-way bulbs.

Electricity is usually carried to houses on overhead wires, resulting in more weather related power failures, often called power *outages*, though it does cut distribution costs. High tension lines are supported by *towers*, or quite commonly, tall poles. All houses are equipped with two 120 volt lines in opposing phases. This enables 240 volts to be used for appliances, such as, hot water heaters, kitchen stoves and dryers. These plugs and outlets are not the same as the 120 volt plugs and outlets. Light switch positions are down for off, up for on.

In Britain electricity comes to the house through underground wires at 240 volts on one phase. Light switches go down for on, up for off. Electrical outlets are usually paired side by side. The *earth* pin on plugs is larger and longer than the other pins, and as it enters the matching hole in the socket, it raises the cover over the other two pins, permitting them to go in. All appliances are either earthed or are double insulated for safety. Light bulbs have a bayonet fitting. The support towers which carry power across the country at high voltages are known as *pylons*. The supply to the house is referred to as the *mains*. Hence a small appliance may be either battery or *mains* operated.

The word *mains* is not used or understood in the U.S. for electricity in the house, or for water or gas supplies. (See EXPLANATIONS on p.167)

# INSTITUTIONS AND SERVICES

*R*athcr than presenting a table of British English / American English comparisons, I have chosen to give a brief description of various institutions, introducing British / American differences with the use of italics.

## THE POSTAL SYSTEM

### The British Postal Service

The postal service in Britain is known as the Royal Mail, and the monarch's head appears on every stamp. The postman comes twice a day on foot in the cities and suburbs. When he has finished the first dclivery known as a *round* he goes back to the post office for the second delivery mail. He wears a navy blue and red uniform.

Letters can go first or second class. The stamps for first class mail are more expensive, but speed the mail along. Second class mail may take a few days. House numbers progress in numerical order, with even numbered houses on one side of the street and odd numbered houses on the other. If an additional mailing address is required, a letter A is added to the nearest house number. Mail within Britain is called *inland* mail.

The *postcode* was devised around 1970 and consists of a combination of letters and numbers such as AB2 2BA. This goes on the last line of the address. It is similar to the American *zip code.*

Mail that has the postage imprinted on it by machine is known as *franked* mail. In the U.S. this is called *metered* mail. If a record of the receipt of the letter is required, one asks for *recorded delivery.*

### The U.S. Postal Service

The American postman, known more commonly in the United States as the mailman or mail carrier, wears a blue uniform which in the summer may consist of a short sleeve shirt, short trousers, and knee socks. Mail delivery is much the same as in Britain, especially in cities and larger towns. However, in many suburbs and in all rural areas mail carriers drive a white jeep with the steering wheel on the "wrong" side. This enables them to deliver and retrieve mail easily at each house by pulling alongside "mail boxes" set on posts standing at the side of each driveway. Attached to the mailbox is a red piece of metal, commonly called a flag, which is set in a vertical position to indicate that there are letters in the box for the mail carrier to retrieve and post. Because of this system, there are not many public mail boxes available in rural areas. Where available, they are large, blue, free standing metal boxes which have a combination receptacle/door at the top which pulls open. After letters are deposited on the door, it is closed, and the door drops the letter into the box. American mail carriers have a *route*.

To facilitate mail delivery, the ZIP code, an acronym for *Zone Improvement Program*, was introduced in 1959 and is required on each piece of mail. It consists of five numbers, a space, then four numbers. The last four numbers are often omitted, even though they do facilitate the handling of mail within their designated zone. It will soon be compulsory to use all nine numbers. Two letters, indicating the State, precede the zip code. There is only one delivery a day, six days a week. Stamps may be purchased not only at the post office but also at vending machines, though the price is slightly higher. Post office vending machines sell stamps at face value. Most supermarkets also sell stamps. Small post offices abound, just as in Britain, and you rarely have to wait long to be served. Except in large cities, you won't find any glass partition between you and the clerk. This is true for banks as well. If you wish to have a receipt from the party you are mailing to, you must ask to send it *return receipt requested*.

## BANKING

British and American banks do not differ much these days. One big difference is that Americans do a lot of their banking at *"Drive Throughs."* Most banks have several drive through lanes in which a pneumatic cylinder whisks your checks (spelt *cheque* in Britain), papers and money into the bank (though too many coins in the cylinder can produce a rather interesting effect as it climbs up the clear plastic tube.) A short while later the cylinder returns with either money or a deposit slip with a voice through the speaker wishing you a nice day. Remember to put the cylinder back before driving off! A United States driving licence, which has one's photo on it, is often required for proof of identity (I.D.) in the U.S. A British or American tourist will need a passport for proof of identity. Most British credit cards can be used at a cash machine to withdraw dollars, but you will need your PIN number.

Below is a comparison of some American banking terms with some used in Britain.

- A Savings and loan is similar to a British Building society

- A Mutual fund is known in Britain as a Unit trust

- Common stock are known as Ordinary shares

- A Checking account is sometimes called a Current account

- A Savings account is known as a Deposit account

- A Money market account is known as a High interest account

- C.D.'s (Certificates of Deposit) are known as Savings certificates

- A stub on a check is sometimes called a counterfoil in Britain

## THE CURRENCY

### British Money

In Britain all the currency *notes* are of a different size, and the higher the denomination, the larger the note. The notes are also a different color, so they cannot easily be confused. The monarchs head is on every note, the denominations being 5, 10, 20 and 50. The notes are changed every few years and a different design is used to avoid counterfeiting. Guineas, shillings, half crowns, florins, and farthings no longer exist. On February 15th 1971, the pound's equivalent in coins was changed from 20 shillings (with 12 pennies to a shilling), to a decimal system with a 100 pennies to a pound. These pennies were called *new pence*. The traditional shillings and pence had been used since the 11th century.

The current silver coins, have recently changed and have no pet names at this time. A *bob* used to be a shilling, (now worth five pence.) A *tanner* used to be the equivalent of six pence or half a shilling. The halfpenny, pronounced *haypnee* is no longer legal tender, nor is the farthing, a quarter of a penny, which was withdrawn in 1961. A guinea was worth one pound and a shilling, and was used when paying fees to professionals. The plural of penny is *pence*. It is one penny, but two pence, formerly pronounced *tuppence*. The symbol £ stands for pounds, p for pence. The one pound note has been replaced by the pound coin, (except in Scotland, where both the note and the coin are used.) A slang term for a pound is a *quid*. If an article costs £1.65, it would be spoken "one pound sixty five." The pound is also referred to as the pound sterling. Pounds (lbs.) are also a unit of weight in Britain, though the metric system is becoming widely used now.

## American Money

In America, currency notes are called *bills* and are all the same size and color (green,) hence the slang term *greenback*. They differ only in the picture, (mostly former U.S. presidents,) and the denomination, which is written in all four corners It is advisable, therefore, to check carefully the denomination of each bill before spending it. American men often carry their bills in a *billfold*, a type of wallet, or in a *money clip*. The most circulated denominations are one, five, ten, twenty, fifty and one hundred. Very rarely you may come across a two dollar bill. These were originally known as deuces and were reintroduced into circulation in the 1970's, along with a new dollar coin (called the Susan B. Anthony dollar). Although both the two dollar bill and the dollar coin are legal tender, neither are in popular use. In recent years the federal bank has been releasing more of the thousands of Susan B. Anthony dollars that were minted in the 1970's and which replaced the so called "Silver Dollar." They are not popular because of their similarity to the twenty five cent coin. Most will probably wind up in collection jars, but it is unlikely that they will ever be worth more than their face value. Americans tend to be resistant to any change in matters of money, miles or gallons. The four most common coins in use have been around for a long time. The one cent, also called a penny, is similar in color and size to the British penny.

The five cent coin is called a nickel. It is silver in color and is roughly the size of a 20p coin. The dime, worth ten cents, is a tiny silver coin. The twenty-five cent coin is commonly called a quarter, and is the same size and color as the new 10p coin. As in Britain, coins are often referred to as "change." If an article costs $1.65, it would be spoken "a dollar sixty five." The $ symbol comes before the dollar amount, the ¢ symbol is placed after the cents if the amount is under a dollar.

The bills used to have names, often inspired by the roman numerals on the corners. The two was known as a deuce, the five as a fin, the ten as a sawbuck (inspired by the Roman numeral X on each corner, which looks like a sawhorse, also known as a sawbuck in the U.S.), the hundred as a C-note (from the Roman numeral C on each corner.)

## RESTAURANTS

### The American Restaurant

Restaurants are plentiful and quite reasonable in the U.S. Americans tend to eat out more than the British. Very often Americans will give directions using restaurants as landmarks. There are many restaurant chains which will serve the same fare wherever you go. To some, this uniformity may seem boring; to others it may provide a sense of security. Service tends to be good, as food servers rely on tips to make a decent income. Tipping is expected. Fifteen to twenty percent is considered a basic tip throughout most of the United States. The tip is left at the table.

There are quite a few restaurants which serve buffet style meals. Even here, if you are waited on in any way, a tip is appropriate – perhaps ten percent. Salad bars are common and usually are quite extensive. Salad dressings come in many flavors. Often fruit and soup will be served at a salad bar, and even assorted flavored jellies, which in Britain might be considered a dessert. Bean and alfalfa sprouts are commonly served with a salad.

Sandwiches, which are enormous and are often a meal in themselves, are on the menu in many restaurants. They are usually served with a pickle and some chips or crisps (fries or chips). You may state what kind of bread you would like (white, whole wheat, pumpernickel, or rye) and whether or not you would like it toasted. Sandwiches often consist of meat, salad and mayonnaise. A *melt,* such as a *tuna melt,* has melted cheese poured over it. If you see the phrase *à la mode* on the dessert menu, it means "with ice cream." Some of the more interesting food names are "Buffalo Wings", "Sloppy Joe" and "Pigs in a blanket." "Enjoy" is often said by the servers after bringing your meal. It's short for "enjoy your meal." The main course is known as the *entrée,* the starter as the *appetizer,* and the sweet or pudding is only known as *dessert.* The term *jacket potatoes* may not be understood. Ask for *baked potatoes.*

Hot tea is available, but in the South you must specify that you want hot tea, since iced tea is more commonly drunk. Hot tea usually comes as a pot of hot water, a tea bag and a sturdy looking cup. Quite often you will get tiny pre-packaged containers of cream (*half and half*) instead of milk, so remember to specify milk or lemon, as desired. Soft drinks are served with lots of ice, especially in the summer. Root beer is a dark soft drink made with juices extracted from roots, herbs, and bark. A smoothie is a drink of milk with blended fruits, (usually with bananas as a base.)

Americans eat their food with the fork held in the right hand and the tines up. My research failed to uncover the origin of this habit. There are many theories, but my choice is that when the West was wild, it was considered polite to eat without brandishing a weapon in your right hand. What *is* known, is that the fork was not in common use until the last century. Soup spoons tend to be smaller than those used in Britain, and desserts are eaten with a small spoon or a fork. (A dessert spoon is not used as a unit of measure.) Broiled means grilled, broasted means grilled and roasted.

Here are some British / American equivalents:
- cutlery is usually called flatware or silverware in the U.S.
- a serviette is called a napkin
- a salt cellar is called a salt shaker
- the head waiter is known as the maitre d'
- the wine waiter is known as the wine steward

- If you wish to take any food home with you, ask for a box, or a doggy bag, (though this term is dying out.)

- When you are ready for the bill, ask for the check (from the German word zeche).

American food has naturally been influenced by the many ethnic groups that settled in the U.S. Here are some explanations of some strange sounding foods you may see on the menu in America:

| | |
|---|---|
| Apple betty | Apple crumble |
| Bagel: | A bread roll in a doughnut shape. |
| Blackened Food: | Food cooked over a strong flame, very spicy. |
| B.L.T. | A "B.L.T." sandwich is the usual term for a bacon, lettuce and tomato sandwich |
| Bologna: [bo·loh·nee] | Smoked, seasoned sausage |
| Buffalo Wings: | Spicy chicken wings (first named in the Anchor bar, Buffalo, N.Y.) |
| Burrito: [bu·ree·toh] | Meat and salad rolled in a tortilla. (Mexican) |
| Caesar salad: | A salad consisting of romaine lettuce, grated cheese, croutons, anchovies, raw egg and olive oil |
| Chowder: | A thick soup of clams, fish or vegetables usually containing potatoes and milk |
| Club sandwich: | This is a double-decker sandwich filled with meat, (usually chicken or turkey), together with tomato, lettuce and mayonnaise |
| Cobbler: | Fruit with pastry on top, cooked in a low pan |
| Coffee cake: | A flat glazed cake or sweetened bread (no coffee in it) |
| Corn bread: | Bread made from cornmeal, usually baked in small loaves |
| Corned beef: | Beef cured in brine then cooked |
| Crepe: | Pancake. |

| | |
|---|---|
| Dagwood: | This is a thick sandwich filled with different types of meat, some cheese and condiments |
| English Muffins: | Something like a crumpet in appearance, but made from a light dough, usually served toasted at breakfast |
| Fried Eggs: | These are ordered "over easy", "over hard", or "sunny side up |
| Grits: | Corn meal cooked with water, usually served as a side dish at breakfast. (Southern) |
| Gumbo: | A soup thickened with okra pods, usually found in the South |
| Gyro: | A Gyro is sliced beef or lamb served as a sandwich on pita bread |
| Hash Browns: | Shredded or diced potatoes, which are then fried |
| Hoagie / Sub: | Meat and salad in a long bread roll (also known as a Hero) |
| Hush Puppies: | Fried corn meal. (So called because they were originally fed to the dogs to keep them quiet.) |
| Links: | Breakfast sausages. Sausages are also served as patties |
| Lox: | Salmon cured in brine |
| Flapjack: | A thick pancake, quite unlike British flapjack (oats mixed with syrup) |
| Nachos: [nah·chōz] | Fried corn tortilla chips covered with some combination of melted cheese, salsa, or beans |
| Pancakes / Hot Cakes: | These are thick pancakes served for breakfast with butter and syrup |
| Pastrami: | Seasoned smoked beef |
| Pigs In A Blanket: | Frankfurters baked in pastry ./ Sausages rolled in pancakes |
| Pretzel: | Hard dough twisted into a fancy shape, usually served as a snack |

| | |
|---|---|
| Reuben: | This is a grilled sandwich of corned beef, Swiss cheese with sauerkraut usually made with rye bread. (Named after Arnold Reuben Jr. Who owned Reuben's restaurant in New York.) |
| Salisbury Steak: | This is minced steak made into a rectangular patty and covered with gravy |
| Sloppy Joe: | Barbecued beef on an open bun |
| Succotash: | Beans (usually lima beans) and corn served together |
| Sweet roll | A roll made with sweetened dough containing raisins and candied fruit, often topped with icing |
| Taco: [tah·coh] | A Mexican food consisting of minced meat, tomatoes, cheese and onion in a hard crusty case |
| Tamale: [to·mah·lee] | Well seasoned minced meat, packed in cornmeal dough, then wrapped in corn husks and steamed |
| Tortilla: [tor·tee·ya] | Flour or corn pancakes (Mexican) |
| Waffles: | These are made from batter, which is cooked in a waffle iron to give it a honeycomb appearance. Served for breakfast with hot syrup |
| Waldorf salad: | Chopped apple, nuts, and celery mixed with mayonnaise |

### The British Restaurant

British restaurants are more individual than their U.S. counterparts. Tipping is less standardized , and often in a casual restaurant there is a jar for tips at the counter. Fifteen percent would be a generous tip. There are many tea houses in small towns and villages. There one can have *high tea* in the afternoon. This consists of sandwiches scones and perhaps a light cooked meal, usually served with a cup of tea. Sandwiches are usually small with a thin filling. Sherry trifle is sometimes served with high tea. It consists of fruit, sherry soaked sponge cake, and sometimes jelly, topped with a custard sauce.

In a restaurant the entree is often called the main course, and the appetizer the starter. Dessert may be called *sweet* or *pudding*. If you have lunch in a pub you will probably be offered a ploughman's (plowman's) lunch, consisting of a hunk of bread, ham, cheese and some pickles.

British foods are traditional. Here are some explanations of some strange sounding foods you may encounter in Britain:

| | |
|---|---|
| Bangers and mash: | A slang term for sausages and mashed potato |
| Black pudding: | A black link sausage containing pork, suet and pigs blood |
| Bubble and squeak: | Mashed potato and vegetables formed into a patty and fried |
| Corned beef | Processed canned beef |
| Crumpet | Made from a yeast mixture, similar in appearance to an english muffin, but doughy |
| Eccles cakes | A flat cake made of pastry filled with currants |
| Gateau [gă·toh] | Any type of rich cake |
| Lemon curd / Lemon cheese | A preserve made from lemon, eggs, sugar and butter |
| Marmite: | A dark, salty vegetable and yeast extract spread on bread |
| Pease pudding [peez] | Split peas boiled with carrots and onions |
| Pikelet [pīk·let] | Similar to a thin crumpet |
| Ploughman's lunch | Bread, cheese and a pickle or salad, often served in a pub |
| Pork pie: | Minced pork covered in pastry (about the size of a cup cake usually.) It is eaten cold |
| Rissole | Ground meat and spices, covered in breadcrumbs and fried |
| Sago pudding | A dessert similar to tapioca pudding. Made from starch from the Sago palm |

| Scotch egg: | A hard-boiled egg covered in sausage meat and deep fried |
|---|---|
| Spotted dick: | A sponge or suet pudding with currants in it |
| Steak and kidney pudding | Chopped steak and kidney steamed in a pudding basin (bowl) lined with pastry |
| Summer pudding | Bread and fresh fruit allowed to set in a pudding bowl |
| Toad in the hole: | Link sausages baked in a pan of batter |
| Yorkshire pudding: | Batter baked in a flat pan, usually served with roast beef |

## BARS

Beer is not ordered by quantity in the U.S. One asks for beer, either on tap, in a can, or in a bottle. If you do not specify the bartender (usually *barman* in the U.K.) will choose for you. In Britain one orders a pint or half pint. A variety of beer brands are available in most bars in both countries. Most cocktails are pretty international, but you may like to try a local mix. Drinks are ordered *straight up* in the U.S. and *neat* in Britain, if no mixer is to be added. A shandy in Britain is half beer and half orange juice. It is customary to leave the bartender a small tip in the U.S, but not in Britain. Toasts are similar in both countries. In Britain my *shout* means that I'm paying. Americans would say my *round* instead.

### Here are some common American drinks:

- A Daiquiri contains rum and lemon mix

- A Highball contains spirits and water or a soft drink, served in a tall glass

- A Manhattan contains whiskey, sweet vermouth and bitters

- A Piña Colada is made of pineapple juice, rum and coconut

- A Tom Collins contains gin, lemon mix and soda water

- Long Island iced tea is not as innocent as the name might suggest. It is a strong alcoholic drink the color of iced tea containing rum, tequila, gin and vodka

- A Mimosa (champagne and orange juice) is called Buck's Fizz in Britain

## SHOPPING

Many British shops are small individually owned shops, and there maybe accommodations above the shop. VAT tax, similar to sales tax in the U.S., is included in the purchase price. Large American style supermarkets are now very common, sometimes they are built out in the country, so that they can provide sufficient parking space for the customers. It is not usual to have your groceries bagged, though larger supermarkets will now bag groceries on request. Plastic bags are provided for your use however. A canvas awning often extends out from small shops to protect the customers from inclement weather. Shopping hours tend to be shorter than in the U.S., and few shops are open on Sundays except the large supermarkets.

- The register is usually called the till in Britain
- Early closing means a day when shops close in the afternoon
- The high street is the equivalent of the U.S. main street
- Bags of groceries are always referred to as shopping

In America your groceries are bagged for you at the checkout and you may be offered assistance in carrying your groceries to the car. A sales tax, similar to VAT is added at the register to all items, with the exception of unprepared food and medications in some States. This means the price marked on the product is not the price you pay at the register. The amount of this tax, a percentage of the price, varies from State to State and even from county to county. Americans are quite specific about where they are going, when they go shopping. Americans go *grocery shopping* at the *grocery store,* if they are going to the supermarket.

- Fresh foods are found in the *produce* [prōdoos] department
- Milk is found in the dairy *case*
- Butter is sold in *sticks*, with four 4oz sticks in a box.

Soda water is usually known as club soda (which may contain some trace potassium compounds) or seltzer water (pure carbonated water.) A surprising number of English foods may be purchased in American supermarkets.

Shopping Centers (Shopping Malls) are the popular way to shop in the States. With huge parking areas, these may cover several acres and be on several levels. Many items of clothing and shoes are known by different names. Note that shoe sizes are slightly different. In order for the British shopper to find the corresponding size in U.S. made shoes, add a size and a half to women's shoes and a half size to men's shoes. Men's shirts go by the same sizes, though long sleeve shirts have various sleeve lengths. Women's dress sizes are different. A U.K. size 10 is a U.S. size 8 for example. With the arrival of metric sizes in Britain, comparisons will be different.

Factory outlet malls, usually located by highways, are fairly new to the U.S. shopper. They consist of stores selling selected brand names in clothing and household items. Here are some American to British translations:

- a *salesperson* is known as a shop assistant.

- *notions* are known as haberdashery.

- *extra large* or XL clothing is known as *outsize*

## FOOD PRONUNCIATIONS

*Phonetics:* I am using two common symbols to indicate a long or short vowel. "◡" indicates a short vowel as in "hăt". "ˉ" indicates a long vowel as in hāte.

| Word | U.S. Pronunciation | U.K. Pronunciation |
|------|-------------------|-------------------|
| Apricot | **ă**pri·cot | **ā**pri·cot |
| Basil | bā·zil | bă zil |
| Fillet | fil·**lay** | **fill**·et |
| Herb | erb | herb |

| *Word* | *U.S. Pronunciation* | *U.K. Pronunciation* |
|--------|----------------------|----------------------|
| Oregano | or·**eh**·gano | ora·**gah**·no |
| Paprika | pa·**pree**·ka | p**ă**p·rika |
| Pasta | **pah**·sta | p**ă**·sta |
| Tomato | to·**mā**·toh | to·**mah**·toh |

## GROCERIES KNOWN BY DIFFERENT NAMES

In compiling this list of comparisons, I have come across several brand names that are as common as, or more commonly used than the generic name. I felt that it was essential to include these words. No endorsement is intended – or should be interpreted – by the use of these words, which appear in capital letters.

*A plus sign* [+]: after a term indicates that the term is known in both the United Kingdom and the United States.

| *U.S.* | *U.K.* |
|--------|--------|
| Beets | Beetroot |
| Biscuit | Scone |
| Candy apple | Toffee apple |
| Confectioner's sugar 4X powdered | Castor sugar |
| Confectioners' sugar 10 X powdered | Icing sugar |
| Cookie | Biscuit |
| Corned beef | Salt beef |
| Cornstarch | Corn flour |
| Cotton Candy | Candy Floss |
| Crawfish | Crayfish + |
| Cream of wheat | Semolina |
| Cured ham | Gammon |

| U.S. | U.K. |
|---|---|
| Custard | Baked custard |
| Custard sauce | Custard |
| Egg nog + | Egg flip |
| Egg Plant | Aubergine |
| Endive | Chicory |
| Fava bean [**fah**·və] | Broad bean |
| Fish sticks | Fish fingers |
| French Fries / Fries | Chips |
| Ginger snap | Ginger nut |
| Graham crackers (similar) | Digestive biscuits |
| Green onion / Scallion | Spring onion |
| Green plum | Greengage |
| Ground meat | Minced meat |
| Half and half | Cream (single) + |
| Heavy / Whipping cream | Double cream |
| Heel (on end of loaf) | Crust |
| Hot dog (without the bun) | Frankfurter + |
| JELL-O | Jelly |
| Jelly / Jam | Jam |
| Jelly Roll | Swiss Roll |
| Large Zucchini (uncommon) | Marrow |
| Layer cake | Sandwich cake |
| Lima bean [līma] | Similar to the broad bean |
| Liverwurst | Liver sausage |
| Molasses | Treacle |
| Oatmeal | Porridge |
| Pancake syrup (similar) | Golden syrup |
| Patty | Rissole |
| Pickle (dill or sweet) | Pickled gherkin |

| U.S. | U.K. |
| --- | --- |
| Plum pudding + | Christmas pudding |
| Pole beans | Stick beans |
| POPSICLE | Ice lolly |
| Potato Chips | Crisps |
| Pound cake | Madeira cake |
| Roast | Joint |
| Romaine lettuce | Cos lettuce |
| Rutabaga | Swede |
| Seeds / Pits | Pips / Stones (fruit) |
| Self rising flour | Self raising flour |
| Shrimp + | Prawns |
| Snow peas + | Mangetout |
| Soda cracker | Water biscuit |
| Soy beans | Soya beans |
| Stick candy | Rock (seaside) |
| String beans | Runner beans |
| Sucker | Lollipop + |
| Tollhouse cookie / Chocolate chip cookie | Chocolate chip biscuit |
| White or Golden Raisins | Sultanas |
| Wiener | Frankfurter + |
| Zucchini | Courgette |

Squash in Britain is an orange or lemon drink made from mixing a concentrate with water.

## SOME DIFFERENT COOKING MEASUREMENTS

A dessertspoon is unknown as a unit of measure in America. (It is the equivalent of two teaspoonfuls.) A cup as a unit of measure is 8 oz. in the U.S. rather than the British 10 oz, and a pint is 16 oz. in the U.S. rather than the 20oz. pint used in Britain.

## CLOTHING AND SHOES KNOWN BY DIFFERENT NAMES

*A plus sign* [+]: after a term indicates that the term is known in both the United Kingdom and the United States.

| *U.S.* | *U.K.* |
| --- | --- |
| Ascot | Cravat |
| Beaded (dress) | Diamanté |
| Business suit + | Lounge suit |
| Canvas sneakers | Plimsolls / Pumps |
| Collar stay | Collar stiffener |
| Coveralls | Boiler suit |
| Crew neck | Turtle neck |
| Cuffs | Turn ups |
| Derby | Bowler hat |
| Fedora | Trilby |
| Garters | Suspenders |
| Golfing knickers | Plus fours + |
| Hose | Stockings + |
| Inseam | Inside leg |
| Jumper | Pinafore dress |
| Knickers | Knickerbockers |
| Made to order | Bespoke |
| Nightgown | Night-dress |
| Off the rack | Off the peg |
| Oxfords | Brogues |
| Pant suit | Trouser suit |
| Panties | Knickers |
| Pants + | Trousers + |
| Pantyhose | Tights |
| Pumps (for ladies) | Court shoes |

| *U.S.* | *U.K.* |
| --- | --- |
| Raincoat + | Mac / Mackintosh |
| Rubber boots + | Wellingtons |
| Ski mask | Balaclava |
| Snap fasteners | Press studs |
| Sneakers | Trainers |
| Suspenders | Braces |
| Sweater + | Woolly / Jumper |
| Sweater set | Twinset |
| Turtle neck | Polo neck |
| Tuxedo | Dinner jacket |
| Undershirt | Vest |
| Undershorts / JOCKEY shorts | Underpants / Y FRONTS |
| Vest | Waistcoat |

Note that SUSPENDERS, JUMPER, KNICKERS, and VEST have very different meanings in the U.K.

## SCHOOLS

### The British School System

In Britain there are many types of schools. Children may start in kindergarten, also known as *Nursery* school, then go on to *Primary* or *Elementary* school. They then start *Junior* school at the age of seven, where they stay until the age of eleven or twelve. They may also go to a *Preparatory* school, or *Prep* school. Prep schools are privately run. They then proceed to their *High* school which may be a *Comprehensive*, a *Grant maintained* or a *Grammar* school. *Grammar* schools usually have admission exams and may have fees. *Grant maintained* schools are funded by private grants and by the department of education. Comprehensive schools divide pupils of differing abilities into *sets*. Schools funded by the government are known as *State* schools. *Public* schools are elite high schools, and are usually very expensive, contrary to what their name implies, although free scholarships are awarded through academic merit. Prince William currently attends the most famous Public school, Eton. Pupils usually attend a Prep (short for preparatory) school before going to a Public school. The school years are designated by *classes* up to high school, and then by *forms*. The highest level of schooling is 6th form The school system in Britain is historic. Many grammar schools were founded as far back as the sixteenth century, and a few even earlier. Shakespeare went to a grammar school. The school principal is known as the head teacher. The school year is divided into three *terms*. A recess is called a break.

G.S.C.E. Exams are taken at the age of fifteen or sixteen, and "A" Levels, which are required to enter a university are taken at the age of seventeen or eighteen.

Fees are required to attend universities in Britain, although scholarships are available. University degrees are as follows; *First, Upper Second, Lower Second* and *Third*. Students who go on for their Masters or Doctorate, are called *postgraduate* students.

## The American School System

Just as in Britain, the children start in kindergarten or pre-school, if their parents so choose. This is often referred to as *K*, when speaking of the grade. The children start school proper, (first grade) at five or six years of age. This is called *Elementary, Grammar*, or *Grade* school. They stay there until fifth grade, when they are ten or eleven. The younger children are encouraged to bring along to school items of interest, e.g., a caterpillar or butterfly to show the other children. This is called *show and tell*. Of course many more exciting items get taken along.

Many children take advantage of the free school buses During the school year, urban roads are fairly swarming with these yellow buses. Other drivers are required to stop behind *and in front* of the bus when it stops to pick up or drop off children, so this can slow down your commute if you get stuck behind one. In the morning many school children are required to recite the *Pledge of Allegiance*. Prayers are not permitted in public schools; however, some schools have a moment of silence for quiet reflection at the start of the day. The school day starts early and finishes early, sometimes by early afternoon. A late student is given a *tardy slip*. A break is known as a *recess*. There are private schools and *academies*, some of which resemble the British Public Schools. Universities and colleges are not free; but scholarships are available for the some students. Americans call any learning establishment "school," which can be confusing. The academic year is divided into two terms called *semesters*.

Pupils (often called *students*) normally progress a grade each year; but if they fail their exams, (*get a failing grade*), then their G.P.A. (*Grade Point Average*) is not high enough and they must repeat a grade. Middle School starts at sixth grade and high school at ninth grade. At the end of the twelfth grade, if they have sufficient credits, they graduate. High school graduation is a big event for American school children. It is marked with a ceremony which is an important right of passage for all young adults. There is also a "*prom*" or formal dance in the senior year. High School Graduation is roughly the equivalent of G.S.C.E., and the S.A.T. (Scholastic Assessment Test, which was known for many years as the Scholastic Aptitude Test) is the equivalent of "A" levels. In high school and college (university) the first year students are called Freshmen, the second year, Sophomores, the third year, Juniors, and the final year, Seniors. The head teacher is known as the *principal*. A *letter jacket* is a windcheater style of jacket with the initial or initials of a school or college on the front. The word student, which is reserved for universities in British English, is used in a broader sense in the U.S. and covers anyone studying. An unexpected test is called a *pop quiz*.

## Comparison of university terms

University terms are very different. Here is a comparison of terms

| U.S. term | U.K. term |
| --- | --- |
| Assistant professor | Lecturer |
| Associate professor | Senior lecturer |
| Commencement | Graduation |
| Dormitory | Hall of residence |
| Full professor | Professor |
| Graduate student | Postgraduate student |
| Instructor | Junior lecturer |
| Major in (a subject) | Read (a subject) |

| **U.S. term** | **U.K. term** |
| --- | --- |
| Pony | Crib |
| President | Vice chancellor |
| Review | Revise |

In the U.S. a *frat house* is a residential house for members of a *fraternity*. This is a social organization of male students, having a name composed of Greek letters. Female students have a *sorority*. These organizations usually have secret rites and one must take a pledge to belong.

U.S. university degrees are as follows: *Cum laude, Magna cum laude, Summa cum laude* (*Summa cum laude* being the highest.)

# THE POLITICAL SYSTEMS

## The U.S. Political System

Legislative bills are presented to the president after being passed by Congress. He has the option of signing the bills, (or certain parts of them) into law or vetoing them. If he let's a bill sit on his desk for ten days (excluding Sundays and legal holidays) without either signing it or vetoing it, the bill automatically becomes law. The president is head of the military and also head of state. His term lasts for four years. Legislation must be approved by the two governing bodies before it reaches the president's desk to be signed into law or vetoed. These governing bodies which are known as *Congress*, consist of the House of Representatives and the Senate. The House of Representatives is often called "the House." The two main parties are the Republicans and the Democrats, which can be compared to the Conservative and Labour parties respectively. The Republicans are often called the G.O.P. (The Grand Old Party.) In the U.S. a candidate *runs* for office.

The two parties are depicted in cartoons by an elephant and a donkey. The elephant represents the Republicans and the donkey represents the Democrats. Each State has two senators, but the number of Representatives is proportional to the particular State's population.

When members of a legislative body get together to decide policy, this meeting is known as a *caucus*. A *plurality* occurs when the winning party has more votes than the other parties, but not a majority.

### The U.K. Political System

The U.K. has a parliamentary system of government. The Members of Parliament are often called M.P.s. (In the U.S. an M.P. is a military policeman.) There are two Houses, the House of Lords and the House of Commons, somewhat like the U.S. Congress. The House of Lords consists of *peers*, men and women who have either been born peers or *raised to the peerage*, which means they have been granted the title through merit. People with a title are collectively known as *peerage*. The House of Commons consists of elected members, who represent their constituency. A *constituency* can also mean a district in Britain as well as a body of voters. A candidate *stands* for office in the U.K. The three main parties are the Conservative party, the Labour party and the Liberal Democrats. Historically the Conservative party is right wing, the Labour party left wing. The Conservatives are also called Tories. The leader of the ruling party is known as the Prime Minister.

### MUSEUMS

There are quite a few differences in pronunciation of terms heard in museums and art galleries. Here is a list of comparisons:

*Phonetics:* I am using two common symbols to indicate a long or short vowel. " ᴗ " indicates a short vowel as in "hăt". " ‾ " indicates a long vowel as in hāte. The letter ə represents an indeterminate vowel sound.

| Word | U.S. Pronunciation | U.K. Pronunciation |
|------|--------------------|--------------------|
| Baroque | barōk | barŏk / barōk |
| Byzantine | biz·ən·teen | bi·zan·tīn |
| Cloche | clōsh | clŏsh |

| *Word* | *U.S. Pronunciation* | *U.K. Pronunciation* |
|---|---|---|
| Dynasty | dĭn·astee | dĭn·astee |
| Huguenot | hyoo·gə·not | hyoo·gə·noh |
| Marie Antoinette | mə·**ree** antwanet | mă̆ree antwanet |
| Van Gogh | van goh | van gof |

A mat around a picture is called a mount in the U.K. A docent is sometimes used for a museum guide in the U.S. For some explanations of art terms see page 175.


## THEATRE

You may wish to take in a show if you are spending time in a big city. The seating is known by different names, so don't be surprised if you are asked if you would like seats in the orchestra in the U.S.! They are referring to the seats at the front. If a play *bombs* in the U.S., it has not gone down well. Quite the opposite meaning of the British expression *"It went like a bomb,"* meaning the play was a hit. The program is sometimes called a *playbill* in the U.S. The break is known as the *intermission,* or just *intermission* (without the article) in the U.S. It is called the *interval* in Britain, where the bar in the theatre is known as a *crush bar,* for obvious reasons. The other U.S. spelling *theater* is no longer as common. The following conversion chart may be helpful.

| *U.S. theatre term* | *U.K. theatre term* |
|---|---|
| Orchestra | Stalls |
| Mezzanine | Circle |
| Balcony | Upper Circle / Balcony |
| Top balcony | Gallery |
| The peanut gallery | The gods |

*English is increasingly being used as a language of communication throughout the world. It has been estimated that up to one and a half billion people on this planet speak English.*

*"Would you like to sit in the stalls Sam ...?"*

(see page 39)

*After the Revolutionary War Americans were
more comfortable with the fact that their English
was different from that spoken in Britain*

# DIFFERENCES IN CUSTOMS AND ETIQUETTE

*T*he United States is a melting pot of nationalities. English may be the national language of the U.S., but many Americans have European, African or Asian ancestors. While we share the same language to a point, American culture is quite different from that of the United Kingdom. Americans use different body language, interact differently and have different customs. Americans will strike up a conversation with a stranger much more readily than a Briton may be accustomed to, and may ask questions that a British person could find a little forward. They often terminate even a brief chat with "Well, it was nice talking to (with) you" or "have a nice day now." Friends and acquaintances greet each other with "Hi" or "Hi there" or "How's it going?" Most Americans answer their phone by just saying "Hello"; whereas most Britons give their name or phone number. On terminating a telephone conversation, an American might say, "Well, I'll let you go now", rather than being blunt and saying, "I have to go now." Americans often give a parting pleasantry, such as "Drive safely" or "Enjoy" that may seem rather like a command to a Briton.

"Thank you" always requires a response in the U.S. The most common response is, "You're welcome." In a casual situation you may hear, "You bet" or "Uh-huh." A Briton might respond with, "Thanks very much", "Not at all" or perhaps, "Cheers" in a casual situation. Sometimes a nod of acknowledgment is considered sufficient response. "Sir" or "Ma'am" is used far more in the U.S. than in Britain. You will hear it often when being served in a restaurant or at some agency. It is also used to catch someone's attention, as in "Sir, you left your keys behind." If an American does not understand you, he or she may simply say "Sir?" or "Ma'am?" This means they want you to repeat your statement or "to run that by them one more time." If you are addressed as "Buster" or "Lady", it is probably not too friendly a form of address, and you have most likely offended the person.

As Henry Higgins put it; an Englishman's way of speaking absolutely classifies him. British culture is of course much older, and in some respects still retains a vestige of life centuries ago. In America, the social pecking order is not apparent merely by accent, though there are exceptions in the large cities. Grammar and word usage however do indicate an American's level of education.

Americans are more inclined to attend church regularly. An estimated 100 million Americans attend a church every Sunday. Synagogues, also called *temples* are also well attended.

Drive ins and Drive throughs are popular in the U.S., especially with banks, though drive in movies have decreased in numbers since the 1980's. The soda fountain (beverage counter) in the local drugstore (general store) has all but disappeared. It was a local meeting point for youngsters in small towns.

Most utility bills (water, electricity, phone, etc.) come monthly in the U.S. They often come only quarterly in Britain. Paid vacations (holidays) are more generous in Britain on the whole. Screens on the windows and central heat and air conditioning are the norm in the southern U.S. Screens are not found on British windows, and though air conditioning is now available in some British cars, private homes almost without exception, do not have air conditioning. Most American cars have air conditioning and automatic transmission. Valet parking is often provided by better American hotels and restaurants, especially in big cities. It is customary to leave a small tip when your car is returned.

Americans have Bigfoot, the British have the Loch Ness monster. Bigfoot, otherwise known as Sasquatch, is a legendary hairy humanoid creature that is said to roam wilderness areas of the U.S., in particular the Pacific Northwest. From time to time people report sightings of this creature.

Foods and eating habits differ. These differences are covered in the section on RESTAURANTS on p.21.


## HEALTH CARE

The British National Health Service does take care of its citizens from cradle to grave, but a patient may have to wait for a non emergency operation. British hospitals where the treatment is free are more austere than American hospitals, but the private hospitals are more comfortable.

There is no national health system in the U.S., but health care is available to all. It is excellent, though very expensive. Those without insurance may have monthly payments to a hospital for many years. Senior citizens are eligible for Medicare, a government health insurance program. The Medicaid program gives indigents health coverage.

## AMERICAN SPORTS

Baseball is the national summer sport. It is played in a *ballpark*, which consists of an *infield* or *diamond* with the bases, and an *outfield* beyond that area. A person who bats both left and right handed is known as a *switch hitter*. Many baseball expressions have made their way into everyday speech. I have listed these further on in the book under IDIOMS AND EXPRESSIONS on p.149; players earn huge sums of money, as do football players. Soccer has become increasingly popular in the U.S. recently. Ice hockey (usually just referred to as hockey) is very popular, and of course football (American style) is a national passion. Fans tend to be reasonably well behaved and rarely get out of control. Football is played on a *gridiron,* presumably because of the appearance of the white lines on the field. The players wear helmets and lots of padding. American football was modeled on the British game of Rugby football. The word *pitch* is unknown in the U.S. for a playing field. The person who throws the baseball however, is known as a *pitcher*. The *World Series* in baseball is similar to a *Test Match* in cricket

## BRITISH SPORTS

Football in Britain is synonymous with soccer. American football is slowly gaining acceptance in and around London. The padding worn by the players is somewhat amusing to the Brits, who can sustain nasty injuries in their games with little body protection. Rugger, or rugby football is closer to American football, where you can run with the ball. A sporting event is called a *fixture* in Britain, and a playing field is also called a *pitch*.

Tennis terms are quite different in Britain. One calls *rough or smooth* to determine the server rather than *up or down*. The *toss* is frequently called the *throw up* in Britain. The call is *'van in'* rather than *'ad in'* after deuce, and before play one has a *knock up* instead of a *warm up*. If the ball falls in the *alley* it is said to have fallen in the *tramlines* in Britain. The terms *fifteen up,* meaning fifteen apiece and *all tied up,* meaning the players are tied, are only used in the U.S. *Australian doubles* or *Canadian doubles* is a tennis game for three players in the U.S.

Cricket is the big summer game in Britain. The *test matches* are the rough equivalent of the *world series* games in the U.S. There are a few cricket terms used in everyday speech in Britain. Well bowled! means Well done! To be *on a good wicket*, means to be in a good position. To be *on a sticky wicket* is not so good. *Knocked for six* means thrown for a loop. Teams played cricket on a regular basis in Central Park, New York years ago, but now baseball has taken over.

## PUBLIC HOLIDAYS

In Britain the *Bank* Holidays are as follows. New Year's Day, Good Friday, Easter Monday, then May Day, which honors the workers, is the first Monday in May. The Spring Holiday occurs on the last Monday in May. In August there is the August Bank Holiday which occurs on the last Monday in August. After Christmas there is Boxing Day. This is the day after Christmas unless Christmas falls on a Saturday, in which case it is celebrated on the following Monday. Mothering Sunday occurs on the fourth Sunday in Lent. This is also known as Mothers Day. Summer Time is the equivalent of Daylight Saving Time in the U.S.

The U.S. has the following *Legal* Holidays. New Year's Day, Martin Luther King Day, which occurs on the third Monday in January, Presidents Day which occurs on the third Monday in February, Memorial Day, formerly Decoration Day, which occurs on the last Monday in May is in remembrance of men and women who were killed in war. It is the unofficial beginning of summer. July 4th is Independence Day which commemorates the adoption of the Declaration of Independence in 1776. It is celebrated with picnics and later, after sunset, with fireworks. Labor Day, which occurs on the first Monday in September is to honor labor and is considered to be the end of summer. Columbus Day, the second Monday in October is celebrated in most States, Veteran's Day is on November 11th.

There is a big celebration at Thanksgiving, another holiday in the U.S. which occurs on the fourth Thursday in November. Thanksgiving Day which became a national holiday in 1863 commemorates the first harvest of the Pilgrim Fathers in America in 1621. It is traditionally celebrated with turkey and pumpkin pie, and is a time of family get-togethers and much feasting. Travel arrangements must be made well in advance if you wish to travel at this time. Christmas decorations usually appear in the shops around this time and sometimes even before.

The American flag is seen flying everywhere all year round, from outside the post offices to the back of a motor cycle. Flags must be illuminated at night, or be taken down. Groundhog Day occurs on February 2nd. According to legend, if the groundhog emerges from hibernation on this day and sees its shadow, there will be another six weeks of winter weather. Mother's Day occurs on the second Sunday in May.

*The internet has been one of the biggest promoters of American English in recent years*

# DRIVING TERMINOLOGY

*T*erminology used in vehicles and on the roads is very different in the two countries. In addition to incorporating some terms while describing driving in the two countries, there is a complete list of term comparisons further on in the book.

## THE BRITISH ROAD

British roads consist of **B** roads, **A** roads and *Motorways*. **B** roads are roughly similar to the American *State Roads*, **A** roads are similar to the American U.S. roads and the *motorways* are similar to the U.S. *Interstate* roads. Motorways all have the designation **M** such as the M25. Apart from driving on the other side of the road, there are several important driving differences. Traffic lights go from red to combined red and amber before turning green. This alerts the driver that the light is about to turn green. Pedestrian crossings with a traffic light are known as *pelican crossings,* from *pe*destrian *li*ght *con*trolled crossing. After red, the traffic light will go to a flashing amber light, which means that pedestrians have the right of way, but the cars may proceed if no one is on the crossing. The traffic light will then turn green, indicating cars may proceed.

You will encounter a round sign on a pole with a black diagonal stripe on a white background. This indicates the end of a speed restriction. The maximum speed in Britain is 70 m.p.h. Seat belts must be worn in both front and rear seats. Signposts do not always give compass directions, so it is advisable to consult the map and note towns and cities through which you will be traveling for reference. It is prohibited to overtake from a slower lane. Yield signs say Give Way.

The motorways have blue signposts, other roads green. The ramps on and off the motorways are known as *slip roads*. Emergency telephones are common on the motorways. Traffic circles are known as *roundabouts* and are very common in Britain. Usually the traffic on the roundabouts has priority over traffic entering. A traffic back up is frequently called a *tailback*. A sign saying *ramp*, indicates there is a difference in the level of the road surface ahead, usually because of construction.

A divided highway is called a *dual carriageway*, and the median is known as the *central reservation*. A green arrow is often called a *filter*. British driving licences do not have a picture of the driver on them at this time, though this may soon change.

## THE AMERICAN ROAD

The *interstates* are the equivalent of the British *motorways*. The slip roads are called *on ramps* and *off ramps*. They tend to be a little shorter, and often lane markings disappear as the slip roads enter the main flow of traffic, which can be disconcerting. Emergency telephones on the interstates are rather sporadic.

The U.S. equivalent of the British **A** and **B** roads are the **US** and **SR** roads. The **US** stands of course, for United States, the **SR** for State Road. The only difference being that the **US** roads continue from one State into the next, whereas the **SR** roads will only take you within the State you are in and are given a different number in the next State. **C** roads, or county roads, tend to have only one lane in each direction and usually are rural. Unlike the British, Americans never use the article with roads. They say, "Take US 27 north", rather than "Take *the* US 27 north."

The center of the U.S. road is marked with yellow lines, white lines are used as lane dividers. In many urban areas over the last twenty years, the central reservation has been made into a turn lane. This keeps the fast lane moving, though occasionally two cars from opposite directions will meet in the middle lane, blocking each others' view. Sometimes the right (slow) lane turns into a right turn only lane, with very little warning, necessitating a fast lane change if you don't want to turn. Overtaking is permitted from a slower lane.

If you encounter a school bus which has stopped to pick up or set down children, you *must* stop, whether you are behind the bus or approaching it on a road without a central reservation known as a *median*, or *median strip*.

Most towns and cities are laid out in a grid pattern. Thus, in some cities or towns, avenues will intersect streets; while in others, numbered streets will intersect named streets with avenues running diagonally through the city. Yet no matter what the variation, there is usually a consistent north-south or east-west direction to all thoroughfares. Accordingly, street addresses are thereby simplified; for example, 2903 14<sup>th</sup> Street West will be very close to the corner of twenty-ninth Avenue and 14<sup>th</sup> St. West. The giving of directions is also simplified; as in, "Go north along 26<sup>th</sup> Street, turn right at the third light, go two blocks then turn left;" or "go north along 26<sup>th</sup> street, turn east at 39<sup>th</sup> Avenue, then north at 19<sup>th</sup> Street." A *block* is often used for measuring distances in a city. It means the distance between streets. Even in the country someone might say; "It's about three city blocks from here."

The term *street* in the U.S. is not restricted to urban areas as it is in Britain. The American equivalent of *high street* is *main street.*

In urban areas, almost every set of traffic lights will include turning arrows which allow for left turns before the on-coming traffic proceeds. Traffic lights are also known as stop lights, red lights, or lights. One set of lights is just known as a *light.* e.g. "Turn at the next light."

## INTERSTATE DRIVING

Driving on the Interstates is very similar to driving on the Motorways. The Interstate signs are shaped like a blue shield with the road number in white letters inside the shield, such as, I-95 or I-4. The even numbered Interstates run east-west, the odd numbered, north-south. Spur roads and orbital roads around large cities will have three numbers, e.g., I-295. Spur roads will start with an odd number, roads that link up with main road at each end will start with an even number. The Interstates have rather infrequent rest areas, which usually consist of toilets (rest rooms), vending machines, and tables and chairs for a picnic. They are generally quite attractive but rarely sell petrol or hot food as do the services in Britain. On some toll roads or turnpikes you will find rest areas with full services. Quite often these are located in the centre of the road (on a large road divider), necessitating an exit from the fast lane. The fastest speed at which you may travel on the Interstates varies from State to State. Occasionally a slip road will lead into the fast lane, which will require your quickly having to attain the speed of the other traffic. The slow lane in the U.S. is known as the *outside* lane; quite the opposite of the slow lane in Britain which is known as the *inside* lane. The reason for the opposite term being used has apparently nothing to do with the fact that the two countries drive on different sides of the road. In South Africa where left hand rule applies on the road, the outside lane is the slow lane.

Speed limits in the U.S. are observed quite well, mainly because the police are very vigilant. The Interstates are patrolled (sometimes from the air) by the highway police of the respective States through which the Interstate runs. These highway patrol officers are also known as State Troopers.

Each State has counties much like British counties. County roads outside the city limits are patrolled by deputy sheriffs (known commonly as *deputies* or *sheriffs*); urban areas by the city police. In some States there are also State police. By the way, if you have ever wondered what the term "Smokey" means, here's the story: "Smokey the Bear" was introduced in a campaign cartoon to educate the public on fire prevention in forests and parks. This bear's big hat resembled that of the State Troopers and before long, the truckers were referring to the State Troopers, as well as any traffic patrol officer, as a "Smokey."

In the U.S. articulated lorries are correctly called *Tractor Trailer Rigs*. The more common terms for large rigs are *eighteen wheelers* or *semis* [semīs]. As they travel the Interstates, they are sporadically required to pull in at Weigh Stations in each State to be weighed. This is for safety reasons. An overloaded truck could be a menace on the roads.

Almost everywhere in the U.S. you can turn right at a traffic light, even if it is red, unless otherwise indicated. You must, of course, stop first to see if it is safe to proceed. In fact, if you are sitting at a traffic light in the right lane with your right turn signal flashing, the car behind you may become impatient if you make no attempt to turn. Sometimes you may see a sign which says "No turn on red," then, of course, you must wait for the light to turn green. This system had been used in certain States for many years, but after the oil crisis in 1973, making a right turn on a red light became almost universal as a means of reducing petrol consumption.

Each State has its own driving (driver's) licence. This is the size of a credit card and has a photograph on the front. They are commonly used for identification purposes, especially when cashing a check and entering a bar. In some States only one number (license) plate at the rear of the car is used.

## RULES OF THE ROAD

Have you ever wondered why Americans drive on the right? The custom probably goes back to the early wagons used in the U.S., where the driver either walked on the left side of the animals which pulled the wagon, or rode on the left rear animal. The reason for this is that most people are right handed, mount a horse from the left and prefer to lead a horse with their right hand. Because of this, the early travelers preferred to keep right, in order to better judge the clearance between passing vehicles. In Britain, wagons were mostly driven from the box with the driver seated on the right, so that he could use the brake and whip with his right hand. Mounting posts for horses were situated on the left side of streets, as horses are mounted on the left side. This resulted in a preference for a keep left rule. European settlers no doubt also influenced the U.S. to keep right and with the arrival of the automobile at the beginning of the twentieth century, the same rules were followed. Curiously the early American cars were right hand drive to help the driver avoid the deep ditches at the sides of the poorly maintained roads, and perhaps to facilitate entering and exiting the car. Interestingly, John McAdam, the inventor of Tarmac constructed a highway that used left hand rule until the mid 1800's. It was called the National Pike, also known as the Cumberland Road and ran from Cumberland, Maryland inland towards Saint Louis, Missouri.

## TERMS FOR THE ROAD (U.K.-U.S.)

*An asterisk* [*]: indicates that further information about a term can be found in EXPLANATIONS on page 167.

*A plus sign* [+]: after a term indicates that the term is known in both the United Kingdom and the United States.

*Square brackets*: indicate the pronunciation of the word.

*Brand Names:* In compiling this lexicon I have come across several brand names that are as common as, or more commonly used than the generic name. Because the brand names may not be understood in the other country, I found it essential to include these words. No endorsement is intended – nor should be interpreted – by the use of these words, which appear in capital letters.

| U.K. Term | U.S. Equivalent |
| --- | --- |
| Accident + | Wreck |
| Articulated lorry | Semi [semī ] / Tractor trailer |
| | Eighteen wheeler |
| Black spot | Accident spot |
| Bollard * | Traffic diverter |
| Bonnet | Hood |
| Boot | Trunk |
| Camper van / DORMOBILE | Conversion van |
| Car park | Parking lot |
| Caravan | Trailer |
| CATSEYES | Reflectors |
| Central reservation | Median / Median strip |
| Chippings | Gravel / Small stones |
| Coach | Tour bus / Motorcoach (rarely spoken) |
| Coupé [coo·pay] | Coupe [coop] |

| U.K. Term | U.S. Equivalent |
|---|---|
| Crash barrier | Guard rail |
| Cut up (someone) | Cut off |
| Derv (**D**iesel **E**ngined **R**oad **V**ehicle) | Diesel fuel for trucks |
| Dipped headlights | Low beam headlights |
| Diversion | Detour |
| Dogleg (in road) | Jog |
| Driving licence | Driver's license |
| Dual carriageway | Divided highway |
| Estate car | Station wagon |
| Excess (on insurance) | Deductible |
| Exhaust pipe + | Tail pipe |
| Filter light | Green arrow |
| Flat battery | Dead battery |
| Flyover | Overpass |
| Gear lever | Gearshift |
| Give way | Yield |
| H.G.V. (Heavy Goods Vehicle) | Semi [semī ] / Eighteen wheeler |
| Hand brake | Parking / emergency brake |
| Hoarding | Billboard + |
| Indicator | Turn signal |
| Juggernaut | Eighteen wheeler |
| Jump leads | Jumper cables |
| Lay-by | Pull off / Turnout (seldom found in U.S.) |
| Lorry | Truck |
| Manual transmission + | Stick-shift |
| Motorway | Interstate / Freeway |
| Mudguard | Fender |

| U.K. Term | U.S. Equivalent |
|---|---|
| Multi-storey car park | Parking garage / Parking ramp (regional N.) / Parking structure (regional W.) |
| Nearside lane / Inside lane | Outside lane (closest to the curb) |
| Number plate | Tag / License plate |
| Offside lane / Outside lane | Inside lane |
| On tow | In tow |
| Overtake + | Pass + |
| Panda car | Police cruiser |
| Pantechnicon [pan·tek·nicon] | Moving van |
| Pavement | Sidewalk |
| Pelican crossing | Pedestrian crossing with lights |
| Petrol | Gas / Gasoline |
| Prang | Fender bender |
| Puncture + | Flat / Flat tire + |
| Ramp | Speed bump + |
| Removal van | Moving van |
| Reverse + | Back up |
| Roadworks | Road construction |
| Roundabout | Traffic circle / Rotary (regional New England) |
| Services | Service area |
| Sleeping policeman | Speed bump + |
| Slip Road | On / Off Ramp |
| Subway | Pedestrian underpass |
| Tailback | Traffic jam + |
| Tailboard | Tailgate |
| Tarmac | Blacktop |
| Third party insurance | Liability Insurance |
| Traffic island | Median |

| U.K. Term | U.S. Equivalent |
|-----------|-----------------|
| Traffic light + | Red light /Stop light / Light |
| Traffic warden | Parking enforcement officer |
| Transport café | Truck stop |
| Unpaved road | Dirt road |
| Verge | Shoulder + / Side median |
| Way out | Exit + |
| Windscreen | Windshield |
| Wing mirror | Side view mirror |
| Zebra crossing | Crosswalk / Pedestrian crossing + |

## TERMS FOR THE ROAD (U.S.-U.K.)

(With some technical terms)

| *U.S. Term* | *U.K. Equivalent* |
| --- | --- |
| Antique car | Veteran car |
| Automobile / Auto (rarely spoken) | Car + |
| Back up | Reverse + |
| Barrel along (colloq) | Belt along |
| Bias ply tires | Cross ply tyres |
| Billboard + | Hoarding |
| Blacktop | Tarmac |
| Body man | Panel beater |
| Boot (wheel immobilizer) | Wheel clamp |
| Break in (engine) | Run in |
| Brights | Main beams |
| Bumper guard | Overrider |
| Carburetor [karburaytor] | Carburettor [karburĕtor] |
| Cattle guard | Cattle grid |
| Conversion van | Camper van |
| Coupe [coop] | Coupé [coo·pay] |
| Crosswalk | Zebra crossing / Pedestrian crossing + |
| Cruiser | Police car + |
| Cut off (someone) | Cut up |
| Dead battery | Flat battery |
| Deadhead, to | To drive without a load |
| Deductible (on insurance) | Excess |
| Detail (clean a car thoroughly) | Valet |
| Detour | Diversion |
| Dimmer switch | Dip switch |

| U.S. Term | U.K. Equivalent |
| --- | --- |
| Dirt road | Unpaved road |
| Divided highway | Dual carriageway |
| Double clutch | Double declutch |
| Drive shaft | Prop shaft |
| Driver's handbook | Highway code |
| Driver's license | Driving licence |
| DUI (Driving Under the Influence) | Drunk driving + |
| Dump truck | Tipper truck |
| Emergency brake | Hand / parking brake |
| Exit + | Way out |
| Fender | Wing / Mudguard |
| Fender bender | Minor traffic accident |
| Fender skirt | Wheel spat |
| Flat | Puncture |
| Four lane highway / Four lane | Dual carriageway |
| Freeway | Motorway |
| Freeze plug | Core plug |
| Gas / Gasoline | Petrol |
| Gas mileage | Fuel consumption + |
| Gas pedal | Accelerator |
| Gearshift | Gear lever |
| Grease fitting | Grease nipple |
| Guard rail | Crash barrier |
| Hairpin curve / turn | Hairpin bend |
| Half shaft | Drive shaft |
| Headliner | Headlining |
| High beam headlights | Main beam headlights |
| High gear | Top gear |
| Hitch | Tow bar |
| Hood | Bonnet |

| U.S. Term | U.K. Equivalent |
| --- | --- |
| In tow | On tow |
| Inside lane | Offside lane / Outside lane |
| Interstate | Motorway |
| Jog (in road) | Dogleg |
| Jumper cables | Jump leads |
| Lemon (car) | Dud / Friday afternoon car |
| Liability insurance | Third party insurance |
| License plate | Number plate |
| Low beam headlights | Dipped headlights |
| Low gear | Bottom gear |
| Lug nut | Wheel nut |
| Make/ Hang a right (left) | Turn right (left) + |
| Median / Median strip | Central reservation / Island |
| Motor home | CARAVANETTE |
| Moving van | Removal van |
| Mudguard | Mudflap + |
| Muffler | Silencer |
| No outlet | No through road + |
| No standing | No stopping |
| Odometer + | Milometer |
| Oil pan | Sump |
| Outside lane (slow lane) | Nearside lane / Inside lane |
| Parking garage / ramp (regional N) / structure (regional W) | Multi-storey car park |
| Parking lights | Sidelights |
| Parking lot | Car park |
| Parkway | Tree lined dual carriageway |
| Patrolman | Police officer |
| Pavement | Road surface |
| Ping | Pink |

| U.S. Term | U.K. Equivalent |
| --- | --- |
| R.V. (recreational vehicle) | CARAVANETTE |
| Rear ended | Hit by the car behind |
| Red light | Traffic light |
| Reflectors | CATSEYES |
| Rest area | Lay-by / Services |
| Rest room | Toilet / Lavatory |
| Road kill | Dead animals on the road |
| Rotary (regional New England) | Roundabout |
| Rumble seat | Dickey seat |
| Sedan | Saloon |
| Semi [semī] | H.G.V./ Articulated lorry |
| Shop | Repair shop |
| Side median | Verge |
| Side mirror / Side view mirror | Wing mirror |
| Sidewalk | Pavement |
| Smokey (slang) | Highway patrol officer |
| Spark plug wires | Spark plug leads |
| Station wagon + | Estate car |
| Stick-shift | Manual transmission + |
| Stop light | Traffic light + |
| Striping the pavement | White lining the road |
| Tag (regional) | Registration sticker / Number plate |
| Tailgate + | Tailboard |
| Tailgate, to | Drive on someone's tail |
| Totaled, was | Is a write off (expressed differently in each country) |
| Traffic circle | Roundabout |
| Trailer | Caravan |
| Trailer hitch | Tow bar |
| Transmission + | Gearbox |

| U.S. Term | U.K. Equivalent |
|---|---|
| Trooper | Highway patrol officer |
| Truck | Lorry / Pick up |
| Trunk | Boot |
| Turning radius | Turning circle |
| Turnout (regional W) | Lay-by |
| Two cycle engine | Two stroke engine |
| Valve cover | Rocker cover |
| Vehicle inspection certificate | M.O.T. certificate |
| Vent window | Quarter light |
| Veteran car | Vintage car |
| Windshield | Windscreen |
| Wreck | Accident + |
| Yield + | Give way |

## PRONOUNCING UK CAR NAMES

| Brand or Model Name | U.K. Pronunciation |
|---|---|
| Datsun | **dăt**·sun |
| Fiat | **fee**·ăt |
| Jaguar | **jag**·u·ah |
| Mazda | **măz**·da |
| Mondeo | mon·**day**·oh |
| Nissan | **nis**·ən |
| Peugeot | **per**·zhoh |
| Renault | **ren**·oh |
| Vauxhall | **vox**·hall |

## PRONOUNCING US CAR NAMES

| *Brand or Model Name* | *U.S. Pronunciation* |
| --- | --- |
| Bonneville | **bonna**·vil |
| Brougham | brome |
| Chevrolet | **shev**·ro·lay |
| Chrysler | crys·ler |
| Ciera | see·**air**·ra |
| Datsun | **daht**·sun |
| De ville | duh·**vil** |
| Fiat | **fee**·aht |
| Galant | ga·**lahnt** |
| Grand Prix | grand pree |
| Hyundai | **hun**·day |
| Jaguar | **jag**·war |
| Marquis | mar·**kee** |
| Mazda | mahz·da |
| Miata | mee·**ah**·ta |
| Nissan | **nee**·sahn |
| Peugeot | pyoo·zhoh |
| Renault | re·**nawlt** |

A B.M.W. car in the U.S. is affectionately called a Beamer   A Mercedes in Britain is sometimes called a Merc.

## RAILWAY (RAILROAD) TERMS

| U.S. Term | U.K. Equivalent |
| --- | --- |
| Box car | Goods wagon |
| Bumpers | Buffers |
| Caboose | Guard's van |
| Car | Carriage |
| Coach (class of travel) | Second class |
| Conductor | Guard |
| Depot [deepoh] | Station + |
| Dining car | Restaurant car |
| Emergency cord | Communication cord |
| Engineer | Engine driver |
| Flat car | Truck |
| Freight car | Goods wagon |
| Freight train | Goods train |
| Grade crossing | Level crossing |
| Layover | Stopover |
| One way ticket | Single ticket |
| Passenger car | Carriage |
| Railroad crossing | Level crossing |
| Round trip ticket | Return ticket |
| Switch - a | Points |
| Switch - to | Shunt |
| Switch tower | Signal box |
| Switchyard | Shunting yard |
| Ticket agent | Booking clerk |
| Ties | Sleepers |
| Tracklayer | Platelayer |

| U.S. Term | U.K. Equivalent |
|-----------|-----------------|
| Track 1 | Platform 1 |
| Train station | Railway station |
| Trestle | Wooden bridge supported by wooden trestles |
| Truck (set of wheels) | Bogie |
| Whistle stop  * | Halt (similar) |

AMTRAK (AMericanTRAvel on tracK) was created by congress in 1970

*As Henry Higgins put it; an Englishman's way of speaking absolutely classifies him.*

*"John, you did ask for some squash didn't you... ?"*

(see page 32)

# PRONUNCIATION

*B*oth Americans and the British, have regional accents. Accent is pronunciation, whereas dialect pertains to grammar and vocabulary. Experts have identified 16 distinct dialect regions in England, and about 26 dialect regions in the United States.

The first pilgrims arrived on the Mayflower in 1620 from Plymouth, England, but most of them were from the Midlands and East Anglia. These colonists would not have sounded their "r"s strongly before a consonant or at the end of a word. They would have said bahn for barn and brutha for brother. When the "r" is sounded, it is called rhotic speech. The pilgrims and subsequent colonists from these parts, presumably are the reason for the non rhotic speech in the New England area today. Other colonists came from the West Country and settled further south. They would have spoken with an accent probably not too unlike the present day accent in the county of Devon, England, which has rhotic speech. This explains the rhotic speech heard in most of the U.S. today.

Most Britons have little difficulty understanding these accents having watched American films, though some of the southern accents are hard even for fellow Americans to understand. Americans have a much more difficult time understanding British speech, so if you want to be understood easily, avoid slang – it is by no means universal – and speak slowly and clearly.

Vowel sounds are quite different. In Britain the "A" in paw, talk, all, etc., is somewhat similar to the vowel sound in pore and lore without the R being sounded. In the U.S. it becomes "AH", resulting in "pah", "tahk", "ahl", etc., except in New Jersey where coffee comes out as cawffee. Also the "O" in hot, top, on, etc. is spoken in British English with rounded lips, quite different from the American "AH" sound. Occasionally, Americans will have difficulty distinguishing between certain words, such as, the names Don and Dawn. To the American's credit they distinguish clearly between talk and torque which is phonetically the same for British people (tawk).

Sometimes in the U.S. the "T" is sounded like a soft "D". Hence thirty, dirty and fruity may sound like "thirdy", "dirdy" and "fruidy". Sometimes the "T" seems to get lost altogether in words like "dentist" and "interesting" which can sound like "dennist" and "inneresting". The "AI" in rain and stain is slightly shorter than its British counter part, as is the "EW" sound in "few" and "grew". In the U.S. the short "A" is used in "chance" and "fast", but it is more drawn out than its counterpart in Northern Britain. Words ending with *ARY, ORY, ERY* are not contracted as they are in British speech. Similarly fruits ending in -berry, such as raspberry and strawberry, are not contracted in American speech. The "O" in words such as orange and Florida, may be pronounced with a short "O" as the British pronounce it, or like the word "or", but this is not consistent. (In Maine the **or** in short sounds like shaht.) Similarly the word "news" may be pronounced nooz or nyooz, though nooz is more common. The U in mutual, cube, butane, Cuba and Houston is a *yoo* sound as it is in British English.

Words such as *tune* and *dual* are sometimes pronounced choon and jewel in British English. In the north of England the "U" sound in putt is almost the same vowel as in put, and book may rhyme with hoot.

The southern States in the U.S., in particular Alabama, Mississippi, Tennessee and Georgia have a distinct accent. The most noticeable characteristic is the long "I", which becomes a drawn out "AH" sound, e.g. wide sounds like wahd. Often the final vowel in a word becomes an indeterminate vowel sound, e.g. Miami sounds like my·**am**·ə. You will frequently hear the expression "Y'all" in the South. This stands for "You all" and is frequently used when addressing more than one person. You-uns is used in the same way in the mid-western States. Another Southern trait is putting emphasis on the first syllable in words such as **en**·tire and **in**·surance.

Aluminum is not only pronounced differently, but it is spelt differently. The name given to the metal by Sir Humphrey Davy was aluminum. It was later changed in Britain to aluminium to conform with the spelling and sound of similar elements in the periodic table, such as Titanium. However, in the U.S. the old form still exists.

The following are some more common words which differ in pronunciation.

*Phonetics:* If a vowel sound cannot be adequately expressed by the use of letters, I have used two common symbols to indicate a long or short vowel. " ◡ " indicates a short vowel as in "hăt". " ‾ " indicates a long vowel as in hāte. If there is no symbol over a vowel, it can be assumed to be a short vowel. An indeterminate vowel sound is expressed by ə. The oo sound as in cook is represented by û.

## SOME PRONUNCIATION DIFFERENCES

| Word | U.S. Pronunciation | U.K. Pronunciation |
|------|--------------------|--------------------|
| Advertisement | adver·**tīz**·ment | ad·**vertis**·ment |
| Agile | **a**·jəl | **a**·jīl |
| Albino | al·**bīn**·ō | al·**bee**·nō |
| Alternate adj., n. | **ault**·ernət | aul·**tern**·et |
| Altimeter | al·**tim**·ə·ter | alti·meeter |
| Anchovy | an·**chō**·vee + | **an**·chə·vee |
| Anti | antī / antee | antee |
| Apparatus | apa·**rătus** | apa·**raytus** |
| Aristocrat | a·**ris**·tocrat | **aris**·tocrat |
| Asphalt | **as′**·fault | **as′**·felt |
| Ate | āte | et |
| Ballet | bal·**ay** | **bal**·ay |
| Banal | **bā**·nəl / banăl | ban·**ahl** |
| baton | bə·**tŏn** | **bă**·ton |
| Been | bin | been |
| Beta | bayta | beeta |
| Bitumen | bī·**too**·men | bĭcher·men |

| *Word* | *U.S. Pronunciation* | *U.K. Pronunciation* |
|---|---|---|
| Brassiere | brə·**zeer** | brăs·eeə |
| Buoy | booee | boy |
| Byzantine | **biz**·an·teen | bi·**zan**·tīn |
| Capillary | **cap**·ilaree | ca·**pil**·əree |
| Caramel | cahr·əmel | căr·əmel |
| Caribbean | kə·**rib**·ēan | karĭ·**bee**·an |
| Carillon | **kari**·lon | kə·**ril**·yon |
| Charade | sha·rād | sha·rahd |
| Chassis | **cha**·see | **sha**·see |
| Chimpanzee | chim·**pan**·zee | chimp·ən·**zee** |
| Clerk | klerk | klark |
| Composite | kəm·**pŏz**·it | **kŏm**·pə·zit |
| Compost | **com**·pōst | **com**·pŏst |
| Conduit | **cŏn**·doo·it | **cŏn**·dit |
| Cordial | **cor**·jəl | cor·dee·al |
| Cremate | **cree**·māte | crə·**māte** |
| Croquet | crō·**kay** | **crō**·kay |
| Cuckoo | koo·koo | kû·koo |
| Cyclamen | **sĭk**·lə·men | **sĭk**·lə·men |
| Dahlia | dă·lee·ə | **dā**·lee·ə |
| Debris | də·**bree** | **deb**·ree |
| Depot | dee·pō / dĕ·pō | dĕ·pō |
| Devolution | dĕva·**loo**·shn | deeva·**loo**·shn |
| Dislocate | dis·**lō**·cate | **dis**·lo·cate |

| Word | U.S. Pronunciation | U.K. Pronunciation |
|------|--------------------|--------------------|
| Docile | dŏ·səl | dō·sīl |
| Double entendre | dubəl on·tahndra | dooblə on·tahndra |
| Dynasty | **dī**·nas·tee | **dĭn**·as·tee |
| En route | en root | on root |
| Err | air | er |
| Figure | figyer / figer | figer |
| Foliage | fō·lē·əj / fō·ləj | fō·lē·əj |
| Forsythia | for·**sĭth**·ēa | for·**sīth**·ēa |
| Fragile | fra·jəl | fra·jile |
| Gala | găla / gāla | gah·la |
| Garage | ga·**rahzh** | garij / **gar**·ahzh |
| Geyser | **gī**·zer | **gee**·zer |
| Glacier | **glay**·sher | **glăs**·ēer |
| Glazier | **glay**·zher | **glay**·zēer |
| Gooseberry | **goos**·bĕree | **gûz**·bəree |
| Hostile | **hos**·təl | hos·tīl |
| Hurricane | hurri·cane | **hurri**·cən |
| Idyllic | ī·dĭllik | ĭdĭll·ik |
| Inquiry | **in**·kwĭ·ree / in·**kwīr** ee | in·**kwīr** ee |
| Interesting | **inter**·esting | **in**·trest·ing |
| Jaguar | **jag**·wah | **jag**·u·ahr |
| Junta | **hûn**·ta | **jun**·ta |
| Khaki | **kă**·kee | **kah**·kee |
| Laboratory | **lab'**·rator·ee | la·**bor**·atree |
| Lasso | la·**soh** | las·**oo** |

| Word | U.S. Pronunciation | U.K. Pronunciation |
|------|--------------------|--------------------|
| Lavatory | lavə·tauree | **lav**·ətree |
| Leisure | lee·zhure | lĕzh·ure |
| Lever | lĕver | leever |
| Lieutenant | loo·ten·ant | lef·ten·ant |
| lilac | lī·lăc | **lī**·ləc |
| Liposuction | līpō·sukshən | līpō·sukshən |
| Literally | **liter**·alee | **lit**·ralee |
| Macho | **mah**·chō | **mă**·chō |
| Mambo | mahm·bo | măm·bo |
| Marquis | mar·**kee** | **mar**·kwis |
| Mauve | mauv / mōv | mōv |
| Migraine | mī·grane | mee·grane |
| Miniature | minē·ăchoor | **min**·əchə |
| Missile | **mis**·əl | mis·ile |
| Mobile | **mo**·bəl | mo·bile |
| Multi | **mul**·tī / **mul**·tee | **mul**·tee |
| Myopic | mī·**ōp**·ic | mī·**ŏp**·ic |
| Omega | ō·**may**·gə | ō·məgə |
| Ordinarily | ordi·**nar**·ilee | **ordin**·erilee |
| Paparazzi | papa·**rah**·tsi | papa·**răt**·see |
| Papier maché | pāp·er **ma**·shay | păp·ēay **mash**·ay |
| Pecan | pə·cahn | pē·căn |
| Perfume | per·**fume** | **per**·fume |
| Premature | prē·mə·**t(y)oor** | **prĕ**·mə·tyoor |

| *Word* | *U.S. Pronunciation* | *U.K. Pronunciation* |
|---|---|---|
| Premier | prə·**meer** | **prĕm**·Iə |
| Primarily | prī·**mar**·ilee | **prī**·mĕrəlee |
| Privacy | **prī**·vasee | **prĭ**·vasee |
| Process | prŏ·sess | prō·sess |
| Progress | prŏ·gress | prō·gress |
| Python | pī·thŏn | **pī**·thən |
| Quinine | kwī·nīn | **kwĭ**·neen |
| Ration | răshən / rāshən | răshən |
| Recluse | **rĕc**·loos | re·**cloos** |
| Renaissance | rena·sens | re·**nay**·sens |
| Reveille | rĕv·alee | rə·vălee |
| Route | rout / root | root |
| Salve | săv | sălv |
| Samba | sahm·ba | sam·ba |
| Saucepan | saus·păn | saus·pən |
| Schedule | **sked**·ule | **shed**·ule |
| Semi | semī | semee |
| Shallot | shălot | shə·**lot** |
| Shone | shŏn | shŏn |
| Solder | sodder | sōlder |
| St. | saint | snt |
| Status | stătus | stātus |
| Strychnine | **strik**·nīn | **strik**·neen |
| Tarpaulin | tar·pə·lin / tar·**pau**·lin | tar·**pau**·lin |

| Word | U.S. Pronunciation | U.K. Pronunciation |
| --- | --- | --- |
| Temporarily | temp·or·**ari**·lee | **temp**·orilee |
| Thorough | thu·rō | thu·ra |
| Trauma | trah·ma | trau·ma |
| Trespass | tres·pass | **tres**·pəs |
| Vase | vās (vahz if over $50) | vahz |
| Vitamin | vī·tamin | vĭ·tamin |
| Vivacious | vī·**vā**·shas | vĭ·**vā**·shas |
| Wrath | răth | rŏth |
| Z | zee | zed |
| Zenith | zē·nith | zĕn·ith |

## SOME NAMES WITH DIFFERENT PRONUNCIATIONS

| Word | U.S. Pronunciation | U.K. Pronunciation |
| --- | --- | --- |
| Bernard | ber·**nard** | **ber**·nəd |
| Cecil | cēcil | cĕcil |
| Marie | mə·**ree** | **mah**·ree / mă·ree |
| Maurice | mau·**rees** | moris |
| Michel | mĭ·**shel** | **mee**·shel |
| Notre Dame | nōter dame | nŏtra dahm + |
| Renee | rə·**nay** | **rĕ**·nay |
| St Augustine | saint **aug**·usteen | st au·**gus**·tin |
| Van Gogh | van·goh | van·gof |

In general words with a French origin are pronounced with the emphasis on the second syllable, e.g. café is pronounced ka·**fay**. The past tenses of the verbs to dive, to fit and to spit, are usually *dove, fit* and *spit,* in the U.S., rather than *dived, fitted and spat* in British English. The past participles of the verbs *to get* and to *mow* are *gotten* and *mowed* respectively in the U.S. rather than got and mown in British English. Lighted is more commonly used than lit, when used as an adjective in the U.S., e.g. a lighted cigarette.

## SOME SPELLING DIFFERENCES

The lexicographer Noah Webster is responsible for many of the differences in U.S. spelling. His *American Dictionary* which came out in 1828 became the standard for U.S. spelling. He originally wanted the U.S. to use completely phonetic spelling, but later compromised with only minor modifications. British spelling has also undergone spelling reform since 1828; most notably terror and horror have lost their -our endings. The -ise suffix is relatively new to British spelling (see below)

| *U.S.* | *U.K.* |
| --- | --- |
| Abridgment | Abridgement |
| Adapter | Adaptor |
| Aging | Ageing |
| Aluminum | Aluminium |
| Ameba | Amoeba + |
| Analyze | Analyse |
| Anesthetic | Anaesthetic |
| Appall | Appal |
| Arbor | Arbour |
| Ardor | Ardour |
| Armor | Armour |
| Armorer | Armourer |
| Armory | Armoury |
| Artifact | Artefact |
| Behavior | Behaviour |

| U.S. | U.K. |
|------|------|
| Behoove | Behove |
| Caliper | Calliper |
| Calisthenics | Callisthenics |
| Canceled / Cancelled | Cancelled |
| Candor | Candour |
| Catalog | Catalogue |
| Center | Centre |
| Chamomile | Camomile |
| Check | Cheque (bank) |
| Chili | Chilli |
| Clamor | Clamour |
| Clangor | Clangour |
| Clarinetist | Clarinettist |
| Color | Colour |
| Color | Colour |
| Counselor | Counsellor |
| Cozy | Cosy |
| Curb | Kerb (on a street) |
| Czar | Tsar |
| Daydream | Day-dream |
| Defense | Defence |
| Demeanor | Demeanour |
| Dependent | Dependant |
| Dialing | Dialling |
| Diarrhea | Diarrhoea |
| Disk | Disc |
| Distill | Distil |
| Dolor | Dolour |
| Doodad | Doodah |
| Draft | Draught |

| U.S. | U.K. |
|---|---|
| Dreamed + | Dreamt |
| Dry-dock | Dry dock |
| Enamor | Enamour |
| Endeavor | Endeavour |
| Enroll | Enrol |
| Enthrall | Enthral |
| Favor | Favour |
| Favor | Favour |
| Favorite | Favourite |
| Favoritism | Favouritism |
| Fervor | Fervour |
| Fiber | Fibre |
| Flavor | Flavour |
| Fulfill | Fulfil |
| Furor | Furore |
| Gage | Gauge + |
| Glamor, | Glamour |
| Gray | Grey + |
| Harbor | Harbour |
| Harbor | Harbour |
| Honor | Honour |
| Honor | Honour |
| Humor | Humour |
| Inquiry | Enquiry |
| Installment | Instalment |
| Instill | Instil |
| Jeweler | Jeweller |
| Jewelry | Jewellery |
| Judgment | Judgement |
| Labor | Labour |

| U.S. | U.K. |
| --- | --- |
| License | Licence |
| Maneuver | Manoeuvre |
| Misdemeanor | Misdemeanour |
| Mold | Mould |
| Mom | Mum |
| Mustache | Moustache |
| Naught | Nought |
| Neighbor | Neighbour |
| Neighbor | Neighbour |
| Neighborhood | Neighbourhood |
| Odor | Odour |
| Pajamas | Pyjamas |
| Paralyze | Paralyse |
| Parlor | Parlour |
| Peddler | Pedlar |
| Percent | Per cent |
| Persnickety | Pernickety |
| Pickanniny | Piccaninny |
| Plow | Plough |
| Practice | Practise |
| Pretense | Pretence |
| Program | Programme |
| Rancor | Rancour |
| Rigor | Rigour |
| Rumor | Rumour |
| Savor | Savour |
| Savory | Savoury |
| Skeptic | Sceptic |
| Skillful | Skilful |
| Spilled | Spilt |

| *U.S.* | *U.K.* |
| --- | --- |
| Splendor | Splendour |
| Story | Storey (of a building) |
| Succor | Succour |
| Sulfur | Sulphur |
| Theater / Theatre | Theatre |
| Tire | Tyre |
| Traveler | Traveller |
| Tumor | Tumour |
| Valor | Valour |
| Vapor | Vapour |
| Vigor | Vigour |
| Vise | Vice (tool) |
| Willful | Wilful |
| Worshiper | Worshipper |

The above spelling is the preferred spelling as recommended in the Oxford English Dictionary and Webster's Dictionary. There are alternative ways of spelling some words.

When adding a suffix to a word in American spelling, remember to double the last consonant only if the stress is on the second syllable of the root word. E.g. *trav·el, traveler* but *pat·rol, patrolling.*

Most words ending in *our* in British spelling end in *or* in American spelling. Words ending with *re* usually end with *er* in American spelling. Theatre is now usually spelt the British way.

The suffix *ize* is preferred by dictionaries in both countries in words such as apologize, finalize, legalize, and realize. Many Britons prefer the *ise* suffix with these words which reflects a French influence on British English since the sixteenth century. The only common words with an s toward the end that U.S. and U.K dictionaries spell differently are: *analyze, cozy* and *paralyze.*

All words which have an **a** followed by an **e** in British English, such as orthopaedics and anaesthesia are spelt without the **a** in American English. Similarly, the **o** is omitted in words such as oedema, oestrogen and oesophagus in American English.

Some words of special interest are those which are spelt with just one different letter or additional letter. These words have both pronunciation and spelling differences.

| *U.K.* | *U.S.* |
| --- | --- |
| Aluminium (alyoo·**min**·eeum) | Aluminum (a·**loo**·minum) |
| Carburettor (karbureta) | Carburetor (karburayter) |
| Divorcee (di·**vor**·see) | Divorcé / Divorcée (di·**vor**·say) |
| Doodah | Doodad |
| Mum | Mom |
| Titbit | Tidbit |

# U.K. - U.S. LEXICON

*A plus sign* [+]: after a term indicates that the term is known in both the United Kingdom and the United States. If this sign is on both the U.S. and U.K. side, the difference is purely in customary word usage.

*An asterisk* [*]: indicates that further information about a term can be found in EXPLANATIONS on page 167.

*Brand Names:* In compiling this lexicon I have come across several brand names that are as common as or more commonly used than the generic names. Because the brand names may not be understood in the other country, I found it essential to include these words. No endorsement is intended – nor should be interpreted – by the use of these words, which appear in capital letters.

*(Colloq.)* indicates the word is used in colloquial speech. A + sign is not used in explaining a colloquial or slang expression, even though the explanation may be known in both countries.

| U.K. Term | U.S. Equivalent |
|---|---|
| Abattoir | Packing house / Slaughter house + |
| Academician | Member of an academy (see academician U.S.) |
| Advert | Ad + |
| Aerial + | Antenna + |
| Aeroplane | Airplane |
| Aggro (colloq.) | Aggravation |
| Agony column | Advice column |
| Air rifle | B B gun / Air gun |
| Allotments | Community gardens |
| Amenity tip / Dump ⊤ | Landfill |
| Amongst | Among + |
| Anti-clockwise | Counter clockwise |

| U.K. Term | U.S. Equivalent |
| --- | --- |
| Appraisal * | Evaluation |
| Approved school (obsolete) | School for delinquent children |
| Arse (vulgar) | Ass |
| Articled clerk | Paralegal (similar) |
| Assault course (military) | Obstacle / Confidence course |
| Assessor (insurance) | Adjuster |
| Assurance | Life insurance |
| Au pair | Young foreign female who helps with children / housework for room and board |
| Autumn + | Fall |
| Banger (dilapidated car) | Heap + |
| Banger (firework) | Firecracker |
| Banger (food) | Sausage + |
| Barmy | Nutty + |
| Barrister | Trial lawyer / Trial attorney |
| Barrow | Pushcart |
| Basin (bathroom) | Sink |
| Bat (table tennis) | Paddle |
| Bath | Bath tub |
| Bathing costume | Bathing suit + |
| Baths | Public swimming pool + |
| Beach hut | Cabana |
| Beaker | Mug (especially a plastic mug) |
| Bedside Table | Night stand |
| Bedsitter | Efficiency apartment |
| Bellboy + | Bellhop |
| Belt along (colloq) | Barrel along |
| Besotted | Smitten + |

| U.K. Term | U.S. Equivalent |
| --- | --- |
| Billion (the U.S. billion is now more common in Britain) | A million million (the U.S. billion is one thousand million) |
| Bird (slang) | Girl |
| BIRO | Ball point pen + |
| Black Maria + | Paddy wagon |
| Blinking (slang) | Goddamn |
| Blind (pull down) | Shade / Window shade |
| Block letters | Capital letters + |
| Block of flats | Apartment building |
| Bloke (slang) | Guy |
| Bloody (slang) | Damn |
| Bloomer (mistake) | Blooper / Boo Boo |
| Bobby | Cop + |
| Boffin | Egghead + |
| Bogey (slang) | Booger [bûger] |
| Boiler (central heating) | Furnace |
| Bollard * | Stanchion / Illuminated traffic diverter |
| Bolt hole | Hideaway + |
| BONIO (dog biscuit) | MILK-BONE |
| Boob (colloq.) | Boo boo |
| Borstal | Reform school + |
| Bottle (fruit) | Can * |
| Bottom drawer | Hope chest |
| Bottom of (street or garden) | Far end of |
| Box spanner | Bone wrench |
| Brilliant (slang) | Great / Cool |
| Bring up + | Raise |
| Bristols (vulgar) | Hooters |

| U.K. Term | U.S. Equivalent |
|---|---|
| Bucket shop (colloq) | Travel agency selling discount travel tickets (see bucket shop U.S.) |
| Budgerigar + | Australian parakeet |
| Building site | Construction site + |
| Bulrush | Cattail |
| Bum (slang) | Butt / Fanny / Buns |
| Bum bag | Fanny pack / Belly or Belt bag |
| Bumf (slang) | Unwanted papers and documents |
| Bun fight (colloq.) | Bash + |
| Bureau | Secretary desk |
| Burgle | Burglarize |
| Busker | Street musician |
| Busy Lizzie (flower) | Impatiens |
| C. V. (Curriculum Vitae) | Résumé |
| C.C.F. (Combined Cadet Force) | R.O.T.C. (Reserve Officers Training Corps) |
| C.I.D. (similar) | F.B.I. |
| Camp bed | Cot |
| Canteen | Cafeteria + |
| Car boot sale | Tailgate sale (not common in the U.S.) |
| Caravan | Trailer / Mobile home |
| Caravan site | Trailer park |
| Carrier bag | Tote bag |
| Carry cot | Bassinet |
| Cash machine | A.T.M. (Automatic Teller Machine) |
| Cashier | Teller in a bank or post office (cashier in other businesses) |

| U.K. Term | U.S. Equivalent |
|---|---|
| Casket | Small ornamental box (see casket U.S.) |
| Casualty (hospital) | Emergency |
| Catapult + | Slingshot |
| Catherine wheel (firework) | Pinwheel |
| Catmint | Catnip + |
| Cattle grid | Cattle guard |
| Catwalk (for modelling clothes) | Runway |
| Chap | Guy * / Fellow + |
| Charity shop | Thrift shop |
| Chartered accountant | C.P.A. (Certified Public Accountant) |
| Chat show | Talk show |
| Cheeky | Nervy / Fresh / Sassy |
| Chemist (person) | Pharmacist + |
| Chemist (shop) | Drug store / Pharmacy + |
| CHOC-ICE | KLONDIKE BAR |
| Christian name | First / Given name |
| Christmas cracker + | Party favor |
| Chuffed (colloq.) | Delighted + |
| Cigarette end | Cigarette butt + |
| Cinema + | Movie theater |
| City centre | Downtown |
| Cling film | SARAN WRAP |
| Cloakroom | Rest room / Checkroom (if used in the literal sense) |
| Clobber (slang) | Clothing / Equipment |
| Clothes peg | Clothes pin |
| Cocktail stick | Toothpick |
| Cold calling | Solicitation |

| U.K. Term | U.S. Equivalent |
| --- | --- |
| Commercial traveller | Traveling salesman + |
| Commis waiter | Busboy |
| Commissionaire | Uniformed doorman |
| Common | Public parkland |
| Compère | M.C. / Master of Ceremonies + |
| Conjurer | Magician + |
| Conkers | Buckeyes |
| Conscription | Draft |
| Constable | Police officer |
| Cooker | Range / Stove + |
| Copper (slang) | Cop + |
| Cordial (drink) | Non alcoholic drink made from fruit juice (see cordial U.S.) |
| Cords | Corduroy pants |
| Corn field * | Wheat field |
| Corner shop | Convenience store |
| Cornet (ice cream) | Cone + |
| Cosh | Club + |
| Costumier | Costumer |
| Cot | Crib |
| Council estate | Public housing project |
| Councillor | Councilman |
| Cowboy (slang) | Disreputable workman |
| Crackers (slang) | Nuts + |
| Cranky | Eccentric (see cranky U.S.) |
| Crazy paving * | Patchwork paved surface |
| Creek | Narrow tidal inlet (see creek U.S.) |
| Creeper | Vine |
| Crematorium + | Crematory [**cree**·matory] |
| Crock (colloq) | Worn out person or thing |

| U.K. Term | U.S. Equivalent |
| --- | --- |
| Crosspatch | Grouch + |
| Cruet | Small container for condiments at the table (see cruet U.S.) |
| Crush barrier | Barricade + |
| CS gas | MACE |
| Cupboard + | Cabinet |
| Cuppa (slang) | Cup of tea |
| Curate | Assistant church minister |
| Curtains + | Drapes / Draperies |
| Cut throat razor | Straight razor |
| Cut up (colloq.) | Upset / Distressed (see cut up U.S.) |
| Cutlery | Flatware / Silverware |
| Cutting (newspaper) | Clipping + |
| D.I.Y. store | Home improvement store |
| Daft | Dumb |
| Dead-head, to | Remove a faded flower head (see deadhead U.S.) |
| Death duties | Estate taxes |
| Decorator | House painter + |
| Diddle (slang) | Cheat |
| Digs (colloq.) | Student accommodations (see digs U.S.) |
| Dinner jacket | Tuxedo / Tux |
| Dishy (colloq.) | Cute + |
| Dismantle + | Disassemble |
| Disorientated | Disoriented |
| Do up | Make over / Do over |
| Dodgy | Uncertain / Risky |
| Doggo (colloq.) | Motionless / Uncooperative |

| U.K. Term | U.S. Equivalent |
| --- | --- |
| Dogsbody | Gofer / Gopher |
| Dole | Unemployment |
| Domestic science | Home economics / Home ec. + |
| Donkey work | Grunt work |
| Doodah | Doodad |
| Dormitory | Room used for sleeping (see dormitory U.S.) |
| Dormitory suburb | Bedroom suburb |
| Doss house | Flop house |
| Dotty | Nutty + |
| Double barrelled surname | Hyphenated last name |
| Double saucepan | Double boiler + |
| Drainpipe + | Rain spout / Down spout |
| Draper | Dry goods retailer |
| Draughts | Checkers |
| Dressing gown | Bathrobe |
| Dry goods | Foodstuffs (see dry goods U.S.) |
| Dumbwaiter * | Lazy susan |
| Dummy (for a baby) | Pacifier |
| Dustbin | Trash can / Garbage can |
| Dustbin day | Garbage day |
| Dustcart | Garbage truck |
| Dutch courage | Alcohol induced courage |
| Earth wire | Ground wire |
| Eiderdown | Comforter |
| ELASTOPLAST | BAND AID + |
| Elevenses | Morning tea break |
| Emulsion paint | Latex paint |
| En-suite (a room) | With a bathroom |
| Envisage | Envision + |

| U.K. Term | U.S. Equivalent |
|---|---|
| Estate agent | REALTOR */ Real estate agent |
| Evening classes | Night school |
| Expiry date | Expiration date |
| Fag (colloq.) | Cigarette (see fag U.S.) |
| Fancy (colloq.) | Care for + |
| Father Christmas + | Santa Claus + |
| Fender (on a boat) + | Bumper |
| Fête | Village fair |
| Film + | Movie + |
| Fire (gas / electric) | Heater |
| Fire Brigade | Fire Department |
| Fish slice | Spatula / Pancake turner |
| Fitted carpet | Wall to wall carpet |
| Fixture (sporting) | Sporting event + |
| Fizzy drink | Pop |
| Flagon | Jug (see jug U.K.) |
| Flannel | Wash cloth / Face cloth |
| Flask + | Thermos + |
| Flat | Apartment / Condominium / Condo |
| Flat mate | Room mate |
| Flat-out | All out |
| Flautist | Flutist |
| Flex (electrical) | Cord |
| Flick knife | Switch blade |
| Flipping (slang) | Darn |
| Flutter (colloq.) | Wager |
| Fly-past | Flyover |
| Forthcoming | Upcoming |
| Fortnight | Two weeks |
| Foyer + | Lobby + |

| U.K. Term | U.S. Equivalent |
| --- | --- |
| Free phone | Toll free |
| Freehold | Outright ownership of land |
| French pleat (hair style) | French twist |
| Fresher (university) | Freshman |
| Fringe (hair) | Bangs |
| Frogspawn | Frogs eggs |
| Fruit machine | Slot machine |
| Fug | Stuffy or smoky atmosphere |
| Full stop (punctuation) | Period |
| Funky (alternative meaning) | Cowardly  (see funky U.S.) |
| Gammy (leg) | Game |
| Garden + | Yard * |
| Gasometer | Gas storage facility  (see facility U.S.) |
| Gazump (colloq.) | Raise the price of some real estate after having accepted an offer |
| Gen (slang) | Poop |
| Gin (alternative meaning) | Trap  (see gin U.S.) |
| Girl guide | Girl scout |
| Git (slang) | Jerk |
| Golden handshake | Retirement present (for long service) |
| Good books | Good graces |
| Goods lift | Freight elevator |
| Goose pimples / flesh | Goose bumps + |
| Granny flat | Mother-in-law apartment |
| Greaseproof paper | Wax paper |
| Green card | Motorists international insurance document  (see green card U.S.) |
| Green fingers | Green thumb + |

| U.K. Term | U.S. Equivalent |
| --- | --- |
| Greengroceries | Produce [prō'doos] |
| Greens (slang) | Vegetables |
| Grill + | Broil * |
| Grotty (slang) | Scuzzy + |
| Ground floor | First floor |
| Grub (slang) | Food |
| Guttering | Gutters + |
| Gymkhana | Horse show |
| Half moon glasses | Half glasses |
| Handbag + | Purse / Pocket book |
| Hash # | Pound |
| Hassock | Church kneeling cushion (see hassock U.S.) |
| Head waiter | Maitre d' |
| Headmaster / Headmistress + | Principal |
| Heap of | Bunch of |
| Heath | Open parkland |
| Hedgerow | Row of hedges |
| Hessian | Burlap |
| Hip bag | Belt bag |
| Hire * (something) | Rent |
| Hire purchase, to buy on | Make payments / Installments on. |
| Hive off | Separate from / Break away from |
| Hob | Range top / Stove top |
| Holiday * | Vacation |
| Holiday maker | Vacationer |
| Homely* | Homey (see homely U.S.) |
| Hooter (slang) | Nose |
| HOOVER, to | Vacuum + |
| Horse blinkers | Horse blinders |

| U.K. Term | U.S. Equivalent |
| --- | --- |
| Horse box | Horse trailer |
| Horse riding | Horse back riding |
| Hot flush | Hot flash |
| House builder | Home builder |
| House trained | House broken |
| Ice lolly | POPSICLE |
| Icing + * | Frosting |
| Identification parade | Line up |
| Immersion heater | Hot water heater (electric) |
| Inheritance tax | Estate tax |
| Inland revenue | Internal revenue service (I.R.S.) |
| Insect + | Bug + |
| Inverted commas | Quotation marks + |
| Invigilator (at university exams) | Proctor  (see proctor U.K.) |
| Ironmonger | Hardware dealer |
| Jam jar | Jelly jar |
| Jammy (colloq.) | Lucky |
| Janitor | Caretaker |
| Jemmy | Jimmy |
| Jim-jams (colloq.) | Jammies |
| Job centre | Employment office |
| Joe Bloggs | Joe Blow |
| Joiner | Cabinet maker |
| Jug * | Pitcher |
| Jumble sale | Rummage sale + |
| Kerfuffle | Commotion |
| Kettle | Tea kettle |
| Key money | A month's rent plus deposit |
| Kieselguhr | Diatomaceous earth + |
| Kiosk + | Concession stand |

| U.K. Term | U.S. Equivalent |
|---|---|
| Kip (colloq.) | Sleep |
| Kirby grip | Bobby pin |
| Knacker | Someone who buys old horses for slaughter |
| Knacker's yard (colloq.) | Glue factory |
| Knock up * (colloq.) | Wake up / Warm up (in tennis) / Put together  (see knock up U.S.) |
| Ladder (in stockings) | Run |
| Lady bird | Lady bug |
| Larder | Pantry + |
| Lashings of (colloq.) | Gobs of |
| Launderette | Laundromat |
| Lavatory + | Bathroom / Rest room |
| Lead (electrical) | Cord |
| Lead (for a dog) + | Leash + |
| Leading article | Editorial |
| Lean-to | A building with a sloping roof abutting a larger building  (see lean-to U.S.) |
| Leasehold property | Property that may be bought and sold but is ultimately owned by another party |
| Leery (glance) | Sly / Knowing  (see leery U.S.) |
| Let (property) | Lease / Rent out |
| Letter box | Mail box / Mail drop |
| LIBERTY | A.C.L.U. (American Civil Liberties Union) |
| Lido | Public outdoor swimming pool |
| Lifebelt / Lifebuoy | Life preserver |
| Lift | Elevator |
| LILO [lie·low] | Air mattress + |

| U.K. Term | U.S. Equivalent |
|---|---|
| Lino [lie·noh] (colloq.) | Linoleum |
| Lipsalve | CHAP STICK |
| Litter bin | Trash can |
| Little Bear (constellation) | Little Dipper |
| Local authority | City / County |
| Lodger | Boarder / Roomer |
| Loft | Attic + |
| Long-sighted | Far-sighted |
| Loo (slang) | John |
| Loudhailer | Bullhorn |
| Lounge | Family room |
| Lovebite | Hickey |
| Lucerne | Alfalfa + |
| Lucky dip | Grab bag |
| Luv (slang) | Hon |
| Mac / Mackintosh | Raincoat |
| Mad (hip slang) | Rad |
| Mailshot | Flier (sent through the mail) |
| Main course | Entrée |
| Mains * | Main |
| Maisonette | An apartment with a private front door accessible from the exterior (usually in a two story apartment complex) |
| Maize | Corn |
| Manager (in business) | Vice president |
| Managing director (in business) | President |
| Market garden | Truck farm |
| Marquee * | Large tent (see marquee U.S.) |
| Mate (colloq.) | Man / Bud |

| U.K. Term | U.S. Equivalent |
|---|---|
| Maths | Math |
| MECCANO set | ERECTOR set |
| Megaphone | Bullhorn |
| Methylated spirits / Meths | Denatured alcohol |
| Milk churn | Milk can |
| Milk float | Milk delivery truck |
| Mind the ... | Watch for/ Look out for... |
| Mount (around a picture) | Mat |
| Mouth organ | Harmonica + |
| Muck about (colloq.) | Cut up |
| Muck in (colloq.) | Pitch in |
| Mudguard | Fender |
| Mum | Mom |
| Music hall | Vaudeville |
| Musical box | Music box |
| Mutt (slang) | Dog (see mutt U.S.) |
| NAAFI (Navy, Army, Airforce Institutes) | PX (Post Exchange) (similar) |
| Nail varnish | Nail polish + |
| Nappy | Diaper |
| Naught | Zero |
| Naughts and crosses | Tic-tac-toe |
| Navvy | Laborer on a public project |
| Neat (of a drink) | Straight |
| Nervy | Nervous (see nervy U.S.) |
| Net curtains | Sheer curtains / Sheers |
| New Year's Eve | New Year's (colloq.) |
| Newsagent | Newspaper store / Newsstand + |
| Newsreader | Newscaster |
| Nick (slang) | Steal |

| U.K. Term | U.S. Equivalent |
|---|---|
| Nil | Zero, Zip |
| Nipper (colloq.) | Kid / Young shaver |
| Nissen hut | QUONSET hut |
| Nod (colloq.) | Big shot |
| Normal / Usual + | Regular |
| Nosey parker (slang) | Busy body |
| Nosh (slang) | Food |
| Note (currency) | Bill |
| Old-age pension | Social security (see social security U.K.) |
| O.A.P. (Old Age Pensioner) | Senior citizen + |
| O.N.O. (Or Nearest Offer) | O.B.O. (Or Best Offer) |
| Oblique ( / ) | Slash + |
| Off-licence | Liquor store |
| Oik | Hood / Lout + |
| Old people's home | Old folks home |
| One off | Custom made |
| Ordinary shares | Common stock |
| Outhouse | Shed near or next to a house (see outhouse U.S.) |
| Outsize | Extra large + |
| Overtake + | Pass + |
| P and P (Postage and Packing) | S and H (Shipping and Handling) |
| P.T.O. (Please Turn Over) | (over) |
| Pack (of cards) | Deck |
| Paddle (walk through shallow water) | Wade + |
| Paddling pool | Wading pool |
| Pantomime | Christmas theatrical performance (see pantomime U.S.) |

| U.K. Term | U.S. Equivalent |
| --- | --- |
| Paper round | Paper route |
| Paraffin | Kerosene |
| Paralytic (slang) | Wasted + |
| Parting (in hair) | Part |
| Patience (card game) | Solitaire  (see solitaire U.K.) |
| Pavement | Sidewalk  (see pavement U.S.) |
| Paving stone | Concrete slab / Paver |
| Peaky | Peaked [peekid] |
| Pebble-dash | Pebble-coated stucco |
| Peckish (colloq.) | Hungry + |
| Pelmet | Valance  (see valance U.K.) |
| Pen friend | Pen pal |
| Penny Farthing | High wheeler |
| Pensioner | Senior citizen + |
| PERSPEX | PLEXIGLASS |
| Petrol | Gas / Gasoline |
| Phonograph | Early phonograph using cylinders (see phonograph U.S.) |
| Physiotherapist | Physical therapist |
| Pianola | Player piano |
| Pillar box | Mail box |
| Pin | Straight pin (in New England: common pin) |
| Pissed (vulgar) | Drunk  (see pissed U.S.) |
| Pitch (sporting term) | Field + |
| Pith | Pulp |
| Plait | Braid |
| Planning permission | Permit |
| Plaster (for a wound) | BAND AID + |
| Play up | Act up + |

| U.K. Term | U.S. Equivalent |
| --- | --- |
| Plonk (slang) | Cheap wine |
| Plot + | Lot + |
| Plough, the (constellation) | The Big Dipper |
| Pneumatic drill + | Jackhammer |
| Polystyrene | STYROFOAM |
| Pong | Stink + |
| Pontoon (card game) | Blackjack + |
| Poof / Poofter (offensive slang.) | Fag |
| Post +* | Mail + |
| Postcode | Zip code |
| Pot plant | Potted plant |
| Potter (around) | Putter |
| Pouffe | Hassock |
| Power point | Electrical outlet |
| Pram / Perambulator | Baby carriage / Stroller |
| Prat | Fool |
| Presently | Soon + |
| Press ups | Push ups + |
| Primary school | Grammar / Grade school |
| Prise open | Pry open |
| Prison warder | Corrections officer |
| Proctor | Disciplinary officer at a university (see proctor U.S.) |
| Property | Real estate |
| Prospectus | Brochure (prospectus is only used for finances in the U.S.) |
| Proud (alternative meaning) | Slightly projecting above |
| Pub | Bar + |
| Public telephone box | Payphone + |
| Public transport | Public transportation |

| U.K. Term | U.S. Equivalent |
| --- | --- |
| Pudding basin | Pudding bowl + |
| Punnet | Container for fruit or vegetables |
| Purse | Change purse |
| Push chair | Stroller |
| Pylon | High tension tower |
| Quarter, a + | A fourth |
| Quay | Wharf + |
| Queue up | Line up |
| Quid (slang) | Pound (money) |
| Rabbit on (colloq.) | Rattle on + |
| Racecourse + | Racetrack |
| Rag (colloq.) | Razz |
| Railway | Railroad |
| Randy (slang) | Frisky / Aroused |
| Rasher | Strip of bacon + |
| Rates | Property taxes |
| Ratty (colloq.) | Irritable  (see ratty U.S.) |
| Red Indian | American Indian, Native American |
| Redcap (colloq.) | M.P. (a member of the Military Police)  (see redcap U.S.) |
| Reef knot | Square knot |
| Reel of cotton | Spool of thread |
| Registrar (legal and university) | Senior administrative officer |
| Retirement pension | Social security |
| Return ticket | Round trip ticket |
| Reverse charge call | Collect call |
| Ride on mower | Riding mower |
| Ring up (phone) | Call |
| Rise (in pay) | Raise |
| Road surface + | Pavement |

| U.K. Term | U.S. Equivalent |
|-----------|-----------------|
| Round (delivery) | Route |
| Roundabout (for children) | Merry go round |
| Roundabout (traffic) | Traffic circle / Rotary (New England) |
| Rowlock | Oarlock |
| Rubber | Eraser |
| Rubbish | Garbage / Trash |
| Rug (light blanket) * | Throw / Lap robe |
| Rumbustious | Rambunctious |
| Rumpus | Ruckus |
| Sack, to | Fire / Can |
| Sale, on * | For sale |
| Saleroom | Salesroom |
| Sales talk | Sales pitch |
| Sand pit | Sand box |
| Sanitary towel | Sanitary napkin |
| Scheme (financial) | Plan + |
| Scribbling block | Scratch paper |
| Scullery | Room off a kitchen, for washing dishes |
| Seaside | Beach + |
| Secateurs | Pruning clippers |
| SELLOTAPE | SCOTCH TAPE |
| Semi-detached (house) | Duplex * (similar) |
| Service flats | Apartment hotel |
| Serviette | Napkin + |
| Settee + | Couch / Sofa + |
| Sheltered accommodation | A.C.L.F. |
| Shin up + | Shinny up |
| Shingle * | Beach pebbles  (see shingle U.K.) |

| U.K. Term | U.S. Equivalent |
| --- | --- |
| Shop assistant | Salesperson |
| Shop steward | Labor union representative |
| Shopping centre + | Mall * |
| Shopping trolley | Shopping cart |
| Short sighted (vision) | Near sighted |
| Sideboards | Sideburns + |
| Single ticket | One way ticket |
| Skint (slang) | Broke + |
| Skip | Dumpster |
| Skip, to | To jump rope |
| Skipping rope | Jump rope |
| Skirting board | Baseboard |
| Slate (colloq.) | Criticize (see slate U.S.) |
| Sleeping partner | Silent partner |
| Slice / Fish slice | Spatula / Pancake turner |
| Slim, to | Diet |
| Slog | Trudge + |
| Slot machine | Vending machine + (see slot machine U.S.) |
| Smalls (colloq.) | Underwear |
| Smashing | Awesome / Cool / Neat. |
| Snakes & ladders (game) | Chutes & ladders |
| Snip, a | Snap |
| Social security | Welfare (see social security U.S.) |
| Sod (vulgar) | Son of a bitch |
| Soft drink + | Soda / Pop / Tonic (in Boston) / Coke (in Tennessee and Alabama) |
| Soil + | Dirt |
| Solicitor | Lawyer / Attorney |
| Solitaire | Peg solitaire |

| U.K. Term | U.S. Equivalent |
|---|---|
| Spanner | Wrench + |
| Speciality | Specialty |
| Spectacles + | Glasses +/ Eye glasses |
| Spirits | Liquor + |
| Spitting (rain) | Sprinkling + |
| Spiv | Small time operator / Shyster |
| Sponge bag | Toilet bag |
| Squash (orange) | Diluted cordial |
| State school | Public school |
| STD (Subscriber Trunk Dialling) | Long Distance  (see STD U.S.) |
| Sticker + | Decal [deecal] |
| Still (of a drink) | Non carbonated |
| Stirrer (colloq.) | Troublemaker |
| Stone (weight) | Fourteen pounds weight |
| Stopover + | Layover |
| Straight away | Immediately + |
| Stream + | Creek |
| STRIMMER (string trimmer) | WEED WHACKER |
| Stroke ( / ) | Slash + |
| Student union | Cafeteria and meeting hall at a university |
| Stuffing + | Dressing |
| Subsidence (in the ground) | Depression / Settling |
| Subway | Underpass |
| Superannuation | Pension plan |
| Suppose, I + | I guess + |
| Surname + | Last name + |
| Swallow dive | Swan dive |
| Sweet | Dessert |
| Sweets | Candy |

| U.K. Term | U.S. Equivalent |
|---|---|
| Swish (colloq.) | Fancy / Elaborate |
| Swot for | Bone up on / Study up on |
| Ta (slang) | Thanks |
| Ta ta (slang) | Goodbye |
| Table | Bring forward for discussion at a meeting (see table U.S.) |
| Tap | Faucet |
| Tart (slang) | Hooker |
| Tea towel | Dish towel / Kitchen towel |
| Teat (on a baby's bottle) | Nipple |
| Telegraph pole | Telephone pole |
| Telly (slang) | TV + |
| Terraced House | Row house |
| Terraces (at a sporting event) | Bleachers / Stands + |
| Tick (√) | A check mark |
| Tick, to | Check |
| Till + | Cash register + |
| Timber | Lumber |
| Tin / Tin opener | Can / Can opener + |
| Tip | Dump + |
| Titbit | Tidbit |
| Toady (colloq.) | Brown-noser |
| Toboggan * | Sled |
| Toe-rag | Jerk |
| Toffee nosed (slang) | Stuck up + |
| Toffee-nosed (slang) | Stuck-up |
| Togs (colloq.) | Clothes |
| Toilet | Rest room / Bathroom / Men's room / Ladies' room |
| Tombola | Ticket lottery held at a fair |

| U.K. Term | U.S. Equivalent |
|---|---|
| Top up | Top off / Freshen (for a drink) |
| Torch | Flashlight |
| Tortoiseshell cat | Calico cat |
| Tot up | Add up + |
| Tout | Scalper |
| Towards + | Toward |
| Tower block | High rise + |
| Traffic fine | Ticket |
| Traffic warden | Parking enforcement officer |
| Tram | Street car |
| Tramp + | Bum / Hobo |
| Transfer + | Decal [deecal] |
| Trapezium | Trapezoid |
| Trapezoid | Trapezium |
| Travelling party | Progressive dinner |
| Tread in (dirt) | Track in |
| Tread on + | Step on + |
| Trolley | Cart |
| Trousers + | Pants + |
| Trug | A shallow gardening basket |
| Truncheon | Billy club / Night stick |
| Trunk + (large suitcase) | Steamer trunk |
| Tube (train) | Subway |
| Tuck in (food) | Dig in + |
| Tucker (slang) | Grub + |
| Tumble dryer | Dryer |
| Turf + | Sod + |
| Twice + | Two times |
| Twig (colloq.) | Catch on / Realize |
| Twister (colloq.) | Swindler  (see twister U.S.) |

| U.K. Term | U.S. Equivalent |
|---|---|
| Tyre lever | Tire wrench / Tire iron |
| Undercarriage (on a plane) | Landing gear |
| Underground (train) | Subway |
| Unit trust (financial) | Mutual fund |
| V.S.O. (Voluntary Service Overseas) | Peace Corps |
| Valance (on a bed) | Dust ruffle / Bed skirt |
| Valet, to (a car) | Detail |
| Valuer | Appraiser * |
| Valves (electronic) | Tubes |
| Vet, to | Screen / Scrutinize + |
| Vicar | Minister + |
| Video | V.C.R. / Video tape |
| Visiting card | Calling card |
| Voluntary work | Volunteer work |
| W.C. | Restroom |
| Walking stick + | Cane |
| Warder | Prison officer / Guard |
| Wash up | Wash the dishes (see wash up U.S.) |
| Water pistol + | Squirt gun |
| Weatherboard | Clapboard |
| Wedding ring + | Wedding band |
| Weir (in a river) | Low dam |
| Wellingtons | Rubber boots + |
| Whacked (slang) | Whipped / Beat |
| Whilst | While + |
| Whinge (Slang) | Bitch |
| White horses (on waves) | White caps |
| White spirit | Liquid solvent |

| U.K. Term | U.S. Equivalent |
| --- | --- |
| Wind (flatulence) | Gas |
| Windcheater | Windbreaker |
| Woken | Awakened |
| Wonky (Colloq.) | Unstable |
| Yard * | Paved area around a house (see yard U.S.) |
| Yeti | Bigfoot (similar) |
| Yob / Yobbo | Hood / Lout + |
| Zip | Zipper, Zip (v) |

*Most English speaking people are unaware how great the differences are between British and American English*

# U.S. - U.K. LEXICON

*A plus sign* [+]: after a term indicates that the term is known in both the United Kingdom and the United States. If this sign is on both the U.S. and U.K. side, the difference is purely in customary word usage.

*An asterisk* [*]: indicates that further information about a term can be found in EXPLANATIONS.

*Brand Names:* In compiling this lexicon I have come across several brand names that are as common as or more commonly used than the generic names. Because the brand names may not be understood in the other country I found it was essential to include these words. No endorsement is intended – nor should be interpreted – by the use of these words, which appear in capital letters.

*Do not assume that all Americans will know all the slang or colloquial words listed.*

| U.S. Term. | U.K. Equivalent. |
|---|---|
| A.C.L.F. | Sheltered accommodation |
| A.C.L.U. (American Civil Liberties Union) | LIBERTY |
| Academician | An academic (see academician U.K.) |
| Accommodations | Accommodation |
| Ace, to (colloq.) | Defeat an opponent |
| Adjuster (insurance) | Assessor |
| Airplane | Aeroplane |
| Alternate [**alt'**·ernet] | Substitute (person) + |
| AMTRAK (AMerican TRAvel on tracK) | American passenger train system |
| Antebellum | Pre civil war (1861) |
| Antenna + | Aerial + |
| Antsy (slang) | Restless / Agitated |
| Apartment (for rent) | Flat (to let) |

| U.S. Term. | U.K. Equivalent. |
|---|---|
| Apartment building | Block of flats |
| Apartment hotel | Service flats |
| Appraisal * | Valuation |
| ATM (Automatic Teller Machine) | Cash dispenser |
| Attaboy, an (slang) | Commendation |
| Attitude (slang) | Uncooperative disposition |
| Attorney | Lawyer +/ Solicitor / Barrister |
| Auxiliary (alternative meaning) | An organisation of volunteers |
| Awesome (hip slang) | Mad / Brilliant |
| B B gun / Air gun | Air rifle |
| Baby carriage | Pram |
| Bad-mouth | Criticise someone |
| Baloney (slang) | Codswallop |
| Bangs (on hair) | Fringe |
| Bankroll, to | Give financial support |
| Banner (year) | Outstanding |
| Barber + | Men's hairdresser + |
| Barf (slang) | Vomit |
| Barrel along (colloq) | Belt along |
| Barrio (colloq) | Spanish speaking district of a town |
| Baseboard | Skirting board |
| Bassinet | Carry-cot |
| Bath tub | Bath |
| Bathrobe | Dressing gown |
| Bathroom (in a public building) | Toilet / Lavatory |
| Bayou (regional So) | Marshy inlet |
| Beat (slang) | Whacked |
| Bedroom suburb | Dormitory suburb |
| Bellhop | Bellboy + |
| Belt bag | Bum bag |
| Benefits (job) | Health insurance / Pension |
| Big Dipper (constellation) | The Plough |

| U.S. Term. | U.K. Equivalent. |
|---|---|
| Bikini * | Men's or women's brief swimsuit |
| Billfold | Notecase / Wallet |
| Bills (currency) | Notes |
| Billy club / Night stick | Truncheon |
| Bitch (slang) | Whinge |
| Bleachers | Stands + / Terraces |
| Block | The distance between streets in a city |
| Block party | Neighbourhood party with the street closed to traffic. |
| Blooper (mistake) | Bloomer |
| Blowout (alternative meaning) * | A big party |
| Boarder | Lodger |
| Boardwalk | Wooden walkway |
| Bobby pin | Flat hairpin |
| Bodacious (colloq) | Outstanding |
| Bombed (colloq.) | Failed + |
| Bone up on | Swat for |
| Bone wrench | Box spanner |
| Boo boo (colloq.) | Boob |
| Booger [bûger} (slang) | Bogey |
| Boondocks / Boonies (slang) | The back of beyond |
| Boot camp | Military style basic training camp |
| Braid (hair) | Plait |
| Branch water | Plain water (not carbonated) |
| Break (colloq.) | Reduction / Discount + |
| Breezeway | Covered outdoor passageway |
| Brochure (for institutions) | Prospectus |
| Broil * | Grill + |
| Brown-bagger | Someone who takes their lunch to work |
| Brownstone | A terraced house, fronted with sandstone |

| U.S. Term. | U.K. Equivalent. |
|---|---|
| Bubbler (regional N.) | Drinking fountain + |
| Buck (colloq) | Dollar |
| Bucket shop (colloq) | Disreputable high pressure brokerage firm (see bucket shop U.K.) |
| Buckeyes | Conkers |
| Buffalo (colloq.) | Confuse someone for gain |
| Bug + | Insect + |
| Building site | Vacant lot for building on (see building site U.K.) |
| Bullhorn | Loudhailer |
| Bum | Tramp |
| Bum adj. (colloq.) | Bad |
| Bumper (on a boat) | Fender + |
| Bunch of | Heap of |
| Bungalow | Small, plain one storey house |
| Buns (slang) | Bum |
| Burbs (slang) | Suburbs |
| Bureau | Chest of drawers |
| Burglarize | Burgle |
| Burlap | Hessian |
| Burro | Donkey used as a pack animal |
| Busboy / Busser | Waiter's assistant / Commis waiter |
| Busted | Broken + |
| Butt +(slang) | Bum |
| Button * (with a message) | Badge |
| C.D. (financial), Certificate of Deposit | Savings certificate |
| C.I.A. (Central Intelligence Agency) | Espionage bureau |
| C.P.A. (Certified Public Accountant) | Chartered accountant |
| Cabana | Beach hut |

| U.S. Term. | U.K. Equivalent. |
|---|---|
| Cabinet | Cupboard + |
| Cabinet maker | Joiner |
| Café | Coffee shop or Night-club |
| Cajun | Pertaining to the people of southern Louisiana who came from Arcadia |
| Calico cat | Tortoiseshell cat (similar) |
| Call (phone) + | Ring up |
| Calling card | Visiting card |
| Calliope [ka·lie·ow·pee] | Steam organ |
| Can (slang) | Sack (v.) / The loo (n.) |
| Can * (in a MASON Jar) | Bottle (in a KILNER jar) |
| Can / Can opener + | Tin / Tin opener |
| Candy | Sweets |
| Cane | Walking stick + |
| Canuck (slang) | Canadian / French Canadian |
| Card (someone) | Check someone's age |
| Carnival | Funfair |
| Cart | Trolley |
| Casket | Coffin + (see casket U.K.) |
| Cat house (slang) | Brothel |
| Cattail | Bulrush + |
| Cattle guard | Cattle grid |
| Catty-corner | Diagonally across |
| Chalkboard | Blackboard + |
| Change purse | Purse |
| CHAP STICK | Lipsalve |
| Chaparral (regional S.W) | Tangled brushwood |
| Charley horse | Cramp (in a limb) |
| Check (in a restaurant) | Bill |
| Check mark, a | Tick |
| Check, to (✓) | Tick |
| Checker | Cashier in a supermarket |

| U.S. Term. | U.K. Equivalent. |
|---|---|
| Checkers | Draughts |
| Checkroom | Cloakroom |
| Cherry picker (colloq.) | Hydraulic boom on a truck which raises a person in the air |
| Chew out (colloq.) | Scold / Reprimand |
| Chigger | Harvest mite |
| Chinook [shi·nook] | Warm, dry wind (either side of the Rocky Mountains) |
| Chipper | Chirpy |
| Chopper (colloq.) + | Helicopter |
| Chutes & ladders | Snakes & ladders |
| Circular file (slang) | Waste-paper basket |
| Clapboard | Weatherboard |
| Clear across (colloq.) | All the way across |
| CLOROX | Bleach + |
| Closet | Cupboard + |
| Clothes pin | Clothes peg |
| Clunker (colloq) | Old bomb |
| Co-ed | Female undergraduate |
| Coffee (colloq.) | Social gathering where coffee is served |
| Coffee klatch (colloq.) | Coffee group |
| Colonial | Pertaining to the period when Britain ruled the original 13 colonies |
| Comforter | Eiderdown |
| Commissary (military) | General store |
| Commode (colloq.) | Toilet |
| Complected | Complexioned |
| Concert master | Leading first violin player |
| Concession stand | Snack bar / Kiosk + |
| Condominium */ Condo | Flat |
| Confidence course (military) | Assault course |

| U.S. Term. | U.K. Equivalent. |
| --- | --- |
| Convenience store + | Corner shop |
| Cookout | Barbecue party |
| Cool * (slang) | Super / Brilliant |
| Cooler | Insulated box for keeping food cool |
| Cordial (drink) | Liqueur (see cordial U.K.) |
| Corn (in the field) | Maize |
| Corrections officer | Prison warder |
| Costumer | Costumier |
| Cot | Camp bed |
| Cotton | Cotton wool |
| Coulee (regional W.) | Deep ravine |
| Councilman | Councillor |
| Counter clockwise | Anti clockwise |
| Coyote [kie·oh·tee] | Wild wolflike dog |
| Crack, to (colloq.) * | Open slightly (window or door) |
| Cracker (regional S.E.) | Country bumpkin |
| Cranky | Irritable (see cranky U.K.) |
| Crazy bone (regional) | Funny bone + |
| Crazy quilt * | Patchwork quilt |
| Cream (slang) | Smash up / Beat up |
| Creamer | Cream jug |
| Creek | Stream (see creek U.K.) |
| Crib | Cot (see cot U.S.) |
| Critter | A wild animal |
| Crud (slang) | Grime + |
| Cruet | Glass bottle for vinegar (see cruet U.K) |
| Cuss (slang) | Swear / Curse + |
| Cut up, a (colloq.) | Joker / Buffoon |
| Cut up, to (colloq.) | Muck about (see cut up U.K.) |
| D.A. | District Attorney |
| D.C. | Washington DC |

| U.S. Term. | U.K. Equivalent. |
| --- | --- |
| Dandy | Super / Exceptional |
| Davenport | Large sofa |
| Deadhead, to | To travel without a payload (see deadhead U.K) |
| Debark | Disembark |
| Decal [dee·cal] | Transfer / Sticker + |
| Deck (house / building) | Paved area or wooden platform adjacent to a house or building |
| Deck (of cards) | Pack (of cards) |
| Deductible (insurance) | Excess |
| Den mother | Akela / Cub Scout Leader |
| Denatured alcohol | Methylated spirits / Meths |
| Deputy / Deputy sheriff | County police officer |
| Desk clerk | Receptionist |
| Dessert + | Pudding / Sweet |
| Detail, to (a car) | Valet a car |
| Diaper | Nappy |
| Diatomaceous earth + | Kieselguhr |
| Dicker | Haggle / Bargain |
| Diddle around (colloq.) | Fiddle around / Waste time |
| Digs (colloq.) | Accommodation (see digs U.K.) |
| Dirt (in yard) | Soil + |
| Dis, to (hip slang) | Disrespect / Snub |
| Disassemble | Dismantle + |
| Discombobulated (slang) | Disconcerted |
| Dish towel | Tea towel |
| Dishpan | Washing-up bowl |
| Dishrag | Dishcloth + |
| Disoriented | Disorientated |
| Docent | Guide in a museum / Lecturer |
| Dog (colloq.) | Unattractive person |
| Dog tag | Soldier's identification tag |

| U.S. Term. | U.K. Equivalent. |
| --- | --- |
| Doodad | Doodah |
| Doohickey | Small mechanical object |
| Doozie, a (slang) | Outstanding |
| Dork | Idiot |
| Dormitory | Building used for sleeping (see dormitory U.K.) |
| Double date | Date on which two couples go out for enjoyment together |
| Double saucepan | Double boiler |
| Down spout | Drainpipe + |
| Downer, a | Something depressing |
| Downtown | City centre |
| Draft | Conscript |
| Drag (colloq.) | Race cars, as in a drag race |
| Drapes / Draperies * | Curtains |
| Dresser | Chest of drawers |
| Dressing | Stuffing + |
| Drool + | Slobber + |
| Drug store | Chemist / Pharmacy + (formerly selling snacks and drinks) |
| Dry goods | Fabrics and clothing (see dry goods U.K.) |
| Dude ranch | Cattle ranch for holidaymakers |
| Dumb (slang) | Daft |
| Dummy | Twit |
| Dumpster | Skip |
| Duplex * | Semi detached house |
| Dust ruffle | Valance (see valance U.S.) |
| Eaves trough | Gutter + |
| Ebonics (from Ebony Phonics) | Black speech + |
| Editorial | Leading article |
| Efficiency apartment | Bedsitter / Bedsit |
| Elevator | Lift |

| U.S. Term. | U.K. Equivalent. |
|---|---|
| Emergency (in a hospital) | Casualty |
| English (on a ball) (regional) | Sidespin |
| Envision + | Envisage |
| Eraser | Rubber |
| ERECTOR set | MECCANO set |
| Evaluation | Appraisal * |
| Exclamation point (punctuation) | Exclamation mark |
| Expiration date | Expiry date |
| Eye glasses | Spectacles / Glasses + |
| F.B.I. (similar) | C.I.D. |
| Face cloth | Flannel |
| Facility | Building built for a specific purpose |
| Fag / Faggot (offensive slang.) | Poof / Poofter  (see fag U.K.) |
| Fall | Autumn + |
| Family room | Lounge |
| Fanny (slang) | Bum |
| Fanny pack (colloq.) | Bum bag |
| Far-sighted | Long-sighted |
| Faucet | Tap |
| Favor, to (regional So) | To look like + |
| Felony | Arrestable offence (similar) |
| Fever blister | Cold sore + |
| Fifth (of a gallon) | A bottle of liquor |
| Figure, I | I think |
| Fill out (a form) + | Fill in |
| Fire cracker | Banger |
| Fire department | Fire brigade |
| Fire house | Fire station + |
| Fire truck | Fire engine + |
| Fire, to | Sack |
| Firecracker | Banger |

| U.S. Term. | U.K. Equivalent. |
| --- | --- |
| First floor | Ground floor |
| Fixing to (regional So.) | Intending to /about to |
| Fixings (slang) | Trimmings |
| Flashlight | Torch |
| Flatware | Cutlery |
| Flip-flop (colloq.) | Backward somersault |
| Floor lamp | Standard lamp |
| Flop house | Doss house |
| Flunk (slang) | Fail |
| Flutist | Flautist |
| Flyover | Fly-past |
| Food stamps | Coupons which can be exchanged for groceries (given to the needy) |
| Fourth, a | A quarter + |
| Frappe (regional New England) | Milkshake |
| Freeloader (colloq.) | Sponger + |
| Freight elevator | Goods lift |
| French doors | French windows + |
| French twist (hair style) | French pleat |
| Frog's eggs | Frogspawn |
| Frosting * | Icing + |
| Funky (alternative meaning) | Stinky  (see funky U.K.) |
| Furnace (central heating) | Boiler |
| G.I. (Government Issue) | U.S. soldier |
| Gander (slang) | Dekko |
| Garage sale * | Jumble sale / Rummage sale |
| Garbage | Rubbish / Kitchen waste |
| Garbage can | Dustbin |
| Garbage day | Dustbin day |
| Garbage truck | Dustcart |
| Gas (flatulence) | Wind |
| Gasoline / Gas | Petrol |

| U.S. Term. | U.K. Equivalent. |
|---|---|
| Geek (hip slang) | Dull, studious person |
| Gin (alternative meaning) | A machine for separating cotton from its seeds (see gin U.K.) |
| Girl scout | Girl guide |
| Given name | Christian name |
| Glue factory (colloq.) | Knacker's yard |
| Goddamn (slang) | Bloody / Blinking |
| Gofer / Gopher | General dogsbody |
| Goof off (colloq.) | Slack off |
| Goose bumps + | Goose pimples / Goose flesh |
| Gouge / Price gouging | To over price |
| Grab bag | Lucky dip |
| Grade school | Primary school |
| Grammar school | Primary School |
| Grandfather clause | Exemption because of pre existing circumstances |
| Grandstand, to | Act in a showy way to sway an audience |
| Grease monkey (slang) | Car mechanic |
| Great room | Combined living / dining area |
| Green (slang) | Money |
| Green card | U.S. Permanent resident card (see green card U.K.) |
| Greenback (slang) | A dollar bill |
| Gridiron (sporting term) | Football field |
| Grocery store | Supermarket + |
| Gross (slang) | Disgusting |
| Ground wire | Earth wire |
| Groundhog | Woodchuck |
| Grunt work (colloq.) | Donkey work |
| Gubernatorial | Pertaining to a sate governor |
| Guess, I | I suppose / Imagine + |
| Gurney | Stretcher + |

| U.S. Term. | U.K. Equivalent. |
| --- | --- |
| Half glasses | Half moon glasses |
| Hassock | Pouffe (see hassock U.K.) |
| Haze, to | Bully / Upset |
| Headed for | Heading for + |
| Heater (gas / electric) | Fire |
| Heinie (slang) | Buttocks |
| Heist (slang) | Robbery |
| Hickey | Love bite |
| High roller | Big spender + |
| Hobo | Tramp |
| Hogtied (slang) | Restained / Thwarted |
| Hokey | Not credible / Overly sentimental |
| Hold over | Relic + |
| Holler | Yell + |
| Home builder | House builder |
| Homely | Plain / Ugly |
| Homer (colloq.) | Home run in Baseball |
| Homey (slang) | Mate |
| Hooch (colloq.) | Cheap liquor |
| Hood (colloq.) | Hoodlum / Tearaway |
| Hoosier | Someone from Indiana |
| Hooters (slang) | Women's breasts |
| Hope chest | Bottom drawer |
| Horse blinders | Horse blinkers |
| Horse trailer | Horse box |
| Horseback riding | Horse riding |
| Hot flash | Hot flush |
| Hotdogger (colloq.) | Stunt performer |
| House broken | House trained |
| Human resources | Personnel + |
| Hunker | Crouch + |
| Hutch | Dresser (see dresser U.S.) |

| U.S. Term. | U.K. Equivalent. |
|---|---|
| Hyphenated name | Double barrelled name |
| I.D. | Identification |
| Indian | Red Indian |
| Indian giver | A person who gives a gift, then asks for it back |
| Installment plan | Hire purchase |
| Internal Revenue Service (I.R.S.) | Inland revenue |
| Jackhammer | Pneumatic drill + |
| Jackrabbit | Hare + |
| Jag | Unrestrained expression of emotion |
| Jam, to | Play improvised jazz music |
| Jammies (colloq.) | Jim-jams |
| Java (slang) | Coffee |
| Jelly | Jam + |
| Jemmy | Jimmy |
| Jerk + | Twerp / Idiot + |
| Joe (slang) | Coffee |
| Joe Blow | Joe Bloggs |
| John * (slang) | Loo |
| John Hancock (slang) | Signature + |
| Johnboat | Small, square ended boat |
| Jug * | Large vessel usually with a cap |
| Jump rope | Skipping rope |
| Jump rope, to | Skip |
| Jungle gym | Climbing frame |
| Kerb store (regional) | Corner shop |
| Kerosene | Paraffin |
| Kibbitz (Yiddish slang) | Give unsolicited advice |
| Kibble | Pelleted pet food |
| Kitty-corner | Diagonally across |
| KLONDIKE BAR | CHOC-ICE |
| Klutz (Yiddish slang) | Clumsy person |

| U.S. Term. | U.K. Equivalent. |
| --- | --- |
| Knock up (slang) | Make pregnant |
| Kook (colloq.) | Eccentric or crazy person |
| Ladybug | Ladybird |
| Lanai (regional S.E.) | Screened porch |
| Landfill | Amenity tip / Dump + |
| Landing gear | Undercarriage |
| Lap robe | Rug (light blanket) * |
| Last name + | Surname |
| Latex paint | Emulsion paint |
| Laundromat | Launderette |
| Lavatory | Basin / Washroom |
| Layover | Stopover |
| LAZY BOY | Recliner + |
| Lazy susan | Dumb waiter * |
| Lean-to | A shelter supported at one side by trees  (see lean-to U.K.) |
| Leash + | Lead + |
| Leery | Wary +  (see leery U.K.) |
| Legal holiday | Bank holiday |
| Life preserver | Life buoy |
| Life vest | Life jacket |
| Lightening bug | Fire fly + |
| Limey (slang) | A British person |
| Line up | Queue up |
| Line up (in a jail) | Identification parade |
| Little Dipper (constellation) | Little Bear |
| Loft | An open elevated area above the main level of a building  (see loft U.K.) |
| Lonesome (implies melancholy) | Lonely + |
| Longshoreman | Docker + |
| Lumber | Timber |
| Lush, a | Drunkard |

| U.S. Term. | U.K. Equivalent. |
|---|---|
| M.C. / Master of Ceremonies + | Compère |
| M.P. | Military police / Redcap (see redcap U.S.) |
| MACE | CS gas |
| Mail drop | Letter box |
| Main drag (colloq.) | Main thoroughfare |
| Maitre d' | Head waiter |
| Make out (slang) * | Snog / Get off with s/o |
| Make over | Do up |
| Mall * | A large shopping centre |
| Man, Dude (form of address) | Mate |
| MARCITE | Compound used for surfacing swimming pools |
| Marquee * (see marquee U.K.) | Large outdoor internally illuminated sign (such as seen outside cinemas) |
| Mash (Southern slang) | Press |
| MASONITE | Fibreboard |
| Mat (around a picture) | Mount |
| Math | Maths |
| Maverick | Unbranded calf / Wild character |
| Medicaid * | Health care program for indigents |
| Medicare * | Federal health insurance program |
| Merry-go-round (for children) | Roundabout |
| Midway | Sideshow location at a fairground |
| Milk can | Milk churn |
| MILK-BONE (dog biscuit) | BONIO |
| Misdemeanor | Non-arrestable offence (similar) |
| Mobile home | Caravan |
| Mom | Mum |
| Momentarily | In a moment / For a moment + |
| Monkey wrench (now obsolete) | Spanner |
| Moose | Elk |

| U.S. Term. | U.K. Equivalent. |
| --- | --- |
| Motel | Motor hotel, accessed by an exterior door |
| Mother-in-law apartment | Granny flat |
| Movie theater | Cinema + |
| Mud room | Vestibule used for removing soiled shoes |
| Mulatto [moo·lah·toe] | Person who is part White and part Negro |
| Mums (colloq.) | Chrysanthemums |
| Murphy bed | Foldaway bed |
| Music box | Musical box |
| Muss up | Mess up + |
| Mutt (slang) | Mongrel + (see mutt U.K.) |
| Mutual fund | Unit trust |
| Native American | Red Indian |
| NAUGAHYDE | PVC (fabric) |
| Near sighted | Short sighted |
| Nerd | Boring, studious person / Square |
| Nervy | Cheeky / Bold (see nervy U.K.) |
| New Year's | New Year's Eve |
| Newscaster | Newsreader |
| Night crawler (regional) | Large worm |
| Night school | Evening classes |
| Night stick | Truncheon |
| Nightstand | Bedside table |
| Nipple (on a baby's bottle) | Teat |
| Nix, to | Veto + |
| No-see-ums (regional) | Biting midges |
| Notarize | Certify |
| Notary public / Notary | Person authorised to certify papers |
| O.B.O. (Or Best Offer) | O.N.O. (Or Nearest Offer) |
| Oarlock | Rowlock |
| Obstacle course (military) | Assault course |

| U.S. Term. | U.K. Equivalent. |
| --- | --- |
| Old folks home | Old people's home |
| One way ticket | Single ticket |
| Open house (realtor's term) | House for sale that may be viewed |
| Operator (alternative meaning) | Devious / manipulative person |
| Order of (in a restaurant) | Portion of |
| Ornery (colloq.) | Difficult (person) |
| OSTERIZER | Blender + |
| Ottoman | Footstool + |
| Outhouse | Outside toilet (see outhouse U.K.) |
| Overseas + | Abroad + |
| Pacifier (for a baby) | Dummy |
| Pack rat | Hoarder |
| Package store | Off-licence |
| Packing house | Abattoir |
| Paddle | Spank + |
| Paddle (table tennis) | Bat |
| Paddy wagon | Black Maria + |
| Panhandle | Beg +(in the street) |
| Pantomime | Show performed by a mime artist (see pantomime U.K.) |
| Paper route | Paper round |
| Paraffin | Paraffin wax + |
| Paralegal | Articled clerk (similar) |
| Pardner | Mate |
| Pardon me | Pardon / Excuse me |
| Part (in hair) | Parting |
| Party favor | Christmas cracker |
| Patsy | Sucker + |
| Pavement | Road surface |
| Peace Corps | V.S.O. (Voluntary Service Overseas) |
| Peaked [peekid] | Peaky |

| U.S. Term. | U.K. Equivalent. |
|---|---|
| Peg solitaire | Solitaire |
| Pen pal | Pen friend |
| Penitentiary | Prison + |
| Period (punctuation) | Full stop |
| Permit (for construction) | Planning permission |
| Pesky (slang) | Annoying |
| Phonograph | Gramophone (see phonograph U.K.) |
| Physical therapist | Physiotherapist + |
| Piazza (regional) | Veranda / Porch |
| Picture I.D. | Proof of identity and age with photograph |
| Pin (on lapel) | Badge |
| Pinkie | Little finger |
| Pinwheel (firework) | Catherine wheel |
| Pissed (vulgar) | Furious (see pissed U.K.) |
| Pistol (colloq.) | Lively person |
| Pitcher | Jug (see jug U.S.) |
| Playbill | Theatre programme + |
| Player piano | Pianola |
| Plea bargain | An admission of guilt to a crime in exchange for a reduced sentence |
| PLEXIGLASS | PERSPEX |
| Pocketbook * | Financial resources / Handbag |
| Polack (offensive slang) | Someone from Poland |
| Pollywog (colloq.) | Tadpole + |
| Pop / Pa | Dad + |
| POPSICLE | Ice lolly |
| Pot holder | Oven glove |
| Pound # | Hash |
| Preppy (colloq.) | Smart, young elite |
| Principal | Headmaster / Headmistress + |
| Prioritize (colloq.) | Establish priorities |

| U.S. Term. | U.K. Equivalent. |
|---|---|
| Proctor | Invigilator (see proctor U.K.) |
| Produce [prō·doos] | Greengroceries,(fruit / vegetables) |
| Professor | University lecturer or professor |
| Projects, the (slang) | Council estate |
| Property tax | Council tax / Rates |
| Pry open | Prise open |
| Public housing project | Council estate |
| Public school | State school |
| Public transportation | Public transport |
| Pulp (of fruit) | Pith |
| Punkie | Biting gnat |
| Punkies (regional) | Biting midges |
| Purse | Handbag |
| PX (Post Exchange) | NAAFI (Navy, Army, Airforce Institutes) |
| Q-TIP | Cotton swab |
| QUONSET hut | Nissen hut |
| Quotation marks + | Inverted commas |
| R.O.T.C. (Reserve Officers Training Corps) | C.C.F. (Combined Cadet Force) |
| Racetrack | Racecourse + |
| Rad (hip slang) | Mad / Brill |
| Railroad, to (colloq.) | Coerce |
| Rain check | A postponement ticket or invitation |
| Raise (in pay) | Rise |
| Raised | Brought up + |
| Ramada (regional S.W.) | Shelter with wooden slats or thatched palms for a roof |
| Rambunctious | Rumbustious |
| Range | Cooker / Stove |
| Rap group | Discussion group |
| Rattle on (slang) | Rabbit on / Ramble on |

| U.S. Term. | U.K. Equivalent. |
| --- | --- |
| Ratty (slang) | Tatty (see ratty U.K.) |
| Razz (slang) | Make fun of |
| Real estate | Property |
| REALTOR */ Real estate agent | Estate agent |
| Redcap | Railway porter (see redcap U.K.) |
| Redd up (colloq.) (regional mid-west) | Tidy up |
| Redneck * (colloq.) | Oyk, yobbo |
| Reform school + | Borstal |
| Register (heating or cooling) | Grille controlling air flow into a room |
| Regular | Normal / Usual + |
| Rest room | Toilet / Lavatory |
| Résumé | C.V. (Curriculum Vitae) |
| ROLODEX | Index card holder |
| Rookie (colloq.) | Novice |
| Roomer | Lodger |
| Round trip ticket | Return ticket |
| Route (delivery) | Round |
| Row house | Terraced House |
| Rubber (colloq.) | Condom |
| Rubberneck, to (slang) | Turn and gaze |
| Rubbing alcohol | Isopropyl alcohol |
| Ruckus | Rumpus |
| Rug (slang) | Hairpiece / Toupee |
| Rugrats (derogatory slang) | Children |
| Rumble (colloq.) | Gang fight |
| Run (in hose) | Ladder (in stockings) |
| Runway (for modeling clothes) | Catwalk |
| S and H (Shipping and Handling) | P and P (Postage and Packing) |
| Sailplane | Glider + |
| Sale *, for | On sale |

| U.S. Term. | U.K. Equivalent. |
| --- | --- |
| Salesperson | Shop assistant |
| Salesroom | Saleroom |
| Sand box | Sand pit |
| Sanitary napkin | Sanitary towel |
| Santa Claus + | Father Christmas + |
| SARAN WRAP (plastic wrap) | Cling film |
| Sassy (colloq.) | Cheeky |
| Scalper | Tout |
| Scarf down | Scoff down + |
| Schedule (bus or train) | Timetable + |
| Schlep (regional slang) | Slog/ Trudge / Lug |
| Schnoz (slang) | Nose (especially a large one) |
| School (colloq.) | School, college or university |
| Schoolyard | School playground |
| Scofflaw | A person who disregards the law |
| SCOTCH TAPE | SELLOTAPE |
| Scratch paper | Scribbling block |
| Secretary desk | Bureau |
| Semester | Half of an academic year |
| Shade / Window shade | Blind |
| Shades (hip slang) | Sunglasses |
| Shanty | Shed / Cabin |
| Sharecropper | Tenant farmer who gives a portion of each crop to the landowner in lieu of rent |
| Sheers / Sheer curtains | Net curtains |
| SHEETROCK | Plasterboard + |
| Sheriff | Chief of police (outside city limits) |
| Shill | Participant in a gambling game who is an employee |
| Shingle * | Asphalt or wooden tile / Small sign (see shingle U.K.) |
| Shinny up | Shin up + |

| U.S. Term. | U.K. Equivalent. |
|---|---|
| Shoot! | Darn it! |
| Shop (colloq.) | Workshop / Garage |
| Short order cook | Cook in a basic restaurant |
| Shower (bridal, wedding) | Ladies gift giving party prior to a big event |
| Shtick | Comedian's / Entertainer's routine |
| Shuck (oysters) | Prise open |
| Shut in, a | Housebound person |
| Shyster | Unethical or unprofessional person (often a lawyer) |
| Side (order) | Side dish |
| Sidewalk | Pavement (see pavement U.S.) |
| Silent partner | Sleeping partner |
| Silverware | Cutlery |
| Skillet | Small frying pan |
| Skinny dipping | Swimming nude |
| Skosh (slang) | A small amount |
| Skycap | Airport porter |
| Slamdunk (slang) | Force through v. / Easy victory n. |
| Slash (/) + | Stoke / Oblique |
| Slate | Set down for nomination / Schedule an event  (see slate U.K.) |
| Sled | Toboggan |
| Slew, a | A lot of |
| Slingshot | Catapult + |
| Slot machine | Fruit machine  (see slot machine U.K.) |
| Smarts (colloq.) | Intelligence |
| Smudge pot | Outdoor paraffin heater, used to protect plants from freezing weather |
| Snake oil (colloq.) | Quack remedy |
| Snap, a (colloq.) | Snip |

| U.S. Term. | U.K. Equivalent. |
|---|---|
| Snippy | Curt + / Ratty (see Ratty U.S.) |
| Snowbird (informal.) | A winter vacationer in the South |
| Social security | Old-age pension / Retirement pension (see social security U.K.) |
| Sod | Turf + |
| Soda | Soft drink + |
| Soda fountain | Snack bar in a general store |
| Solitaire | Patience |
| Some (colloq., used at end of sentence) | A little |
| Someplace | Somewhere + |
| Sow bug | Woodlouse |
| Spatula / Pancake turner | Fish slice / Slice |
| Specialty | Speciality |
| SPEEDOS (colloq.) | Brief swimming trunks for men |
| Spigot | Outdoor tap / Stopcock |
| Split, to (slang) | Get moving / Scarper |
| Spooked | Scared + |
| Spool of thread | Reel of cotton |
| Square knot | Reef knot |
| Squirrelly [skwerly] | Eccentric / Capricious |
| Squirt gun | Water pistol + |
| Stand-off | Deadlock + |
| Stateside | In the U.S. |
| STD (Sexually Transmitted Disease) | VD / Venereal disease + (see STD U.K.) |
| Steamer trunk | Trunk + |
| Stiff, to (slang) | Fail to tip s/o |
| Stir crazy (slang) | Restless from confinement |
| Stogy / Stogie | A long, thin, inexpensive cigar |
| Stoked (slang) | Worked up |
| Stool (alternative meaning) | Toilet |
| Stoop | Porch + |

| U.S. Term. | U.K. Equivalent. |
| --- | --- |
| Store | Shop or department store |
| Storm window | Secondary glazing (similar) |
| Stove + | Cooker |
| Straight pin | Pin |
| Straightaway (on a course) | Straight |
| Street car | Tram |
| Stroke (colloq.) | Compliment |
| Stroller | Push chair |
| Studly (hip slang) | Handsome / Macho |
| STYROFOAM | Polystyrene, (expanded) |
| Subway (train) | Underground |
| Surgery, a | Operation + |
| Swale | Marshy depression |
| Swan dive | Swallow dive |
| Swap meet (mostly used in the West) | Sale of old cars and machinery at an outdoor venue / Flea market |
| Swing shift | Evening shift + |
| Switch blade | Flick knife |
| Table (secondary meaning) | Put a bill or motion on one side for future discussion (see table U.K.) |
| Tacky (colloq.) | Tatty / Tasteless + |
| Taffy | Small pieces of seaside rock |
| Tag | Label + |
| Tag (regional) | Number plate / Registration sticker |
| Tag office (regional) | Vehicle licence office + |
| Tag sale | Rummage sale |
| Tailgate sale | Boot sale |
| Talk show | Chat show |
| Tank (regional Texas) | Pond |
| Tarheel | Someone from N. Carolina |
| Tart | Whore |
| Tea kettle | Kettle |

| U.S. Term. | U.K. Equivalent. |
| --- | --- |
| Teamster | Lorry driver |
| Teeter totter | See saw + |
| Telephone pole | Telegraph pole |
| Teller | Cashier (in a bank or P.O.) |
| Temblor | Earthquake + |
| Temple | Synagogue + |
| Thread | Cotton + |
| Thrift shop | Charity shop |
| Through (e.g. Mon through Wed) | Up to and including |
| Throw (light blanket) | Rug * |
| Thumbtack | Drawing pin |
| Tick off | Tell off + |
| Tic-tac-toe | Naughts and crosses |
| Tidbit | Titbit |
| Tightwad | Miserly person |
| Tin ear, a | Tone deaf + |
| Tire wrench | Tyre lever |
| Titled | Entitled + |
| Toilet bag | Sponge bag |
| Toll free | Free phone / Freefone |
| Top off | Top up |
| Totaled (vehicle) | A write off |
| Toward + | Towards + |
| Track in (dirt) | Tread in |
| Trackless trolley | Trolleybus + |
| Trade | Swap + |
| Traffic circle | Roundabout |
| Trailer park | Caravan site |
| Tram | Parking lot conveyance |
| Tramp + | Slut / Down and out |

| U.S. Term. | U.K. Equivalent. |
|---|---|
| Transfer | Ticket permitting a bus or train passenger to change to another vehicle to complete their journey |
| Trapezium | Trapezoid |
| Trapezoid | Trapezium |
| Trash | Rubbish |
| Trash can | Litter bin |
| Trash, to | Destroy + |
| Trip, a (slang) | Experience |
| Trolley | Tram / Bus resembling a cable car |
| Truck farm | Market garden |
| Tube (electronic) | Valve |
| Turkey | Idiot / Loser |
| Turnkey (house or flat) | Fully equipped |
| Turnpike | Toll road + |
| Tuxedo | Dinner jacket |
| Twister (colloq.) | Tornado (see twister U.K.) |
| Two family | A property divided into two residences |
| Uncle Sam | The U.S. government |
| Up (sporting term) | Apiece + |
| Upchuck (slang) | Vomit |
| Upcoming | Forthcoming |
| Utility bills | Electricity / Gas / Water bills |
| V.C.R. | Video (player) |
| Vacation | Holiday |
| Vacationer | Holiday maker |
| Valance | Pelmet (see valance U.K.) |
| Vamoose (slang) | Rush off |
| Vanilla (hip slang) | Ordinary |
| Vanity | Dressing table + |
| Vaudeville | Music hall |
| Veg out [vej] (hip slang) | Loll about |

| U.S. Term. | U.K. Equivalent. |
|---|---|
| Vet * | War veteran / Veterinarian |
| Villa (regional E) | House within a condominium * |
| Vine | Creeper |
| Visit with *(colloq.) | Visit / Chat with |
| Volunteer work | Voluntary work |
| Vo-Tech | Technical Institute |
| W.A.S.P. | White Anglo Saxon Protestant |
| Waitlist, to | Put on a waiting list |
| Walk-up | Above ground flat with no lift |
| Wall to wall carpet | Fitted carpet |
| Wash cloth | Flannel |
| Wash the dishes | Do the washing up |
| Wash up | Wash yourself (see wash up U.K.) |
| Washroom (regional North) | Public toilet |
| Wastebasket | Waste-paper basket + |
| Water cooler | Cold water dispenser |
| Wax paper | Greaseproof paper |
| Wedding band | Wedding ring + |
| Welfare | Social security (see social security U.S.) |
| WEED WHACKER | STRIMMER |
| Wetback (derogatory slang) | Illegal Mexican immigrant |
| Whippoorwill | A variety of nightjar |
| Whistle stop | Small town on a railway line |
| White caps | White horses |
| Windbreaker | Windcheater |
| Wood alcohol | Methanol + |
| Yankee | Someone who lives north of the Mason Dixon line |
| Yard * | Garden (see yard U.K.) |
| Yard man | Gardener |
| Yard work | Gardening |

| U.S. Term. | U.K. Equivalent. |
| --- | --- |
| Yellow jacket | Paper wasp + |
| ZAMBONI | Ice cleaning machine (on a rink) |
| Zero + | Nil / Nought |
| Zip (slang) | Nothing |
| Zip code | Postcode |
| Zipper | Zip |
| Zit | Pimple |

## SOME DIFFERENT TERMS FOR PUNCTUATION

| U.S. Term | U.K. Equivalent |
|---|---|
| [ ]    Bracket + | Square bracket |
| ( )    Parenthesis | Bracket |
| /    Slash + | Stroke, Oblique |
| ✓    Check mark | Tick |
| !    Exclamation point | Exclamation mark + |
| .    Period | Full stop |
| " "    Quotation marks + | Inverted commas |

The decimal point in the U.S. is always a full stop, unlike the British decimal point which is usually positioned half way up the line e.g. (·)

## SOME DIFFERENT FURNISHING TERMS

| U.S Term | U.K. Equivalent |
|---|---|
| Area rug | Rug (large) |
| Baseboard | Skirting board |
| Bassinet | Carrycot |
| Breakfront | Display Cabinet |
| Buffet | Sideboard |
| Bureau | Chest of drawers |
| Cot | Camp bed |
| Couch + | Settee + |
| Credenza [cra·den·za] | Sideboard / Cabinet for papers or supplies in an office |
| Crib | Cot |
| Davenport | Sofa + |

| | |
|---|---|
| Drapes / Draperies * | Curtains |
| Dresser | Chest of drawers (often with a mirror) |
| Dust ruffle | Valance |
| Floor lamp | Standard lamp |
| Hassock | Pouffe |
| Highboy | Tallboy |
| Hutch | Dresser |
| Lowboy | Small dressing table |
| Murphy bed | Foldaway bed |
| Ottoman | Footstool |
| Secretary desk | Bureau / Davenport |
| Sheer curtains / Sheers | Net curtains |
| Side server | Sideboard |
| Trundle-bed | Truckle-bed |
| Valance | Pelmet |

## SOME DIFFERENT TERMS FOR TOOLS

| *U.S. Term* | *U.K. Term* |
|---|---|
| Alligator clip | Crocodile clip |
| Blow torch + | Blow lamp |
| Bone wrench | Box spanner |
| Boot (wheel immobilizer) | Wheel clamp |
| Coping saw | Fretsaw |
| Jackhammer | Pneumatic drill + |
| Monkey wrench | Pipe wrench + |
| Vise (spelling difference) | Vice |
| Wall anchor | RAWLPLUG |
| Wrench | Spanner |

## FUNFAIR (CARNIVAL) TERMS

| *U.K. Term* | *U.S Term* |
| --- | --- |
| Big wheel | Ferris wheel |
| Candy floss | Cotton candy |
| Dodgem cars | Bumper cars + |
| Merry-go-round | Carousel |
| Sideshow location | Midway |
| Steam organ | Calliope [ka·lī·ōpee] |
| Switchback | Roller coaster |
| Toffee apple | Candy apple |

## SOME DIFFERENT GARDENING TERMS

| *U.K. Term* | *U.S Term* |
| --- | --- |
| Busy Lizzie | Impatiens |
| Casuarina | Australian pine |
| Dead-head | Remove dead flower heads |
| Norfolk pine | Norfolk Island pine |
| Secateurs | Pruners / Pruning shears |
| Trug | Shallow gardening basket |

Many plants are pronounced differently. Look under SOME PRONUNCIATION DIFFERENCES

## SOME DIFFERENT MEDICAL TERMS

| *U.S Term* | *U.K. Term* |
| --- | --- |
| Acetaminophen / TYLENOL | Paracetamol (drug) |
| Aide | Auxillary |
| Appendectomy + | Appendicectomy |

| | |
|---|---|
| Anesthesiologist | Anaesthetist |
| Antenatal | Prenatal + |
| Charge nurse | Ward sister |
| Chronic fatigue syndrome + | M.E. (which stands for Myalgic Encephalomyelitis) |
| Circulating nurse | Theatre sister |
| Crib death | Cot death |
| Diaper | Nappy |
| Doctor's office | Doctor's surgery |
| Emergency department | Casualty department |
| I.V. | Drip |
| In isolation | In a barrier / isolation ward |
| Internist | Specialist in internal diseases |
| Lidocaine | Lignocaine |
| M.D. + | G.P. + |
| Mononucleosis + | Glandular fever |
| Operating room | Operating theatre / Theatre |
| Physical Therapist | Physiotherapist |
| Podiatrist | Chiropodist (similar) |
| Resident doctor | Registrar |
| RN + | Sister |
| Scrubs / Scrub suit | Theatre whites / Theatre garb |
| Shot (colloq.) + | Jab |
| Specialist | Consultant (similar) |
| Tongue depressor | Tongue blade |
| Visiting nurse | District nurse |
| Walker | Walking frame / Zimmer frame |

All words which have an **a** followed by an **e** in British English, such as orthopaedics and anaesthesia are spelt without the **a** in American English. Similarly, the **o** is omitted in words such as oedema, oestrogen, foetus and oesophagus in American English.

*Americans comprise seventy per cent of the people who speak English as their first language; however British English is widely taught as a second language*

*"My wife loves pot plants Sam"*

(see page 145)

# WHAT NOT TO SAY

## WORDS AND TERMS THAT A BRITON SHOULD AVOID IN AMERICA

BRILLIANT (slang):  Use GREAT or COOL.

CARRY ON:  Use GO AHEAD or YOU FIRST.

CHEERS:  Use THANKS or GOODBYE if used in a slang sense.

DEAR:  This is not used often in the U.S. for EXPENSIVE.

ESTATE AGENT: Could be misunderstood.  Use REALTOR

FAG:  This is a derogatory term for a gay person in the U.S.  Use CIGARETTE.

FAGGED OUT:  Use BEAT or WHIPPED.

GIVE ME A TINKLE:  Could sound vulgar. Try GIVE ME A CALL instead.

HOMELY:  This means unattractive in the U.S.  Try HOMEY.

I'VE KNOCKED MYSELF UP:  Vulgar in the U.S.  Try I'VE KNOCKED MYSELF OUT

KEEP YOUR PECKER UP:  Vulgar in the U.S.  Try KEEP SMILING.

KNOCK UP:  When playing tennis, use WARM UP

KNOCK ME UP:  A vulgar expression in the U.S.  Try WAKE ME UP.

LAY THE TABLE:  Use instead SET THE TABLE.

MAY I TOP YOU UP?: Would not be understood in the U.S. Try WANT ME TO TOP THAT OFF? Or MAY I FRESHEN YOUR DRINK?

MY MATE: A mate in the U.S. usually refers to a marriage partner. Try MY BUDDY.

NO NAKED LIGHTS: Use NO OPEN FLAMES

POT PLANT: This would mean a marijuana plant to most Americans! Try HOUSE PLANT.

POTTY ABOUT: Would not be understood in the U.S. Try CRAZY ABOUT.

RING ME UP: Use GIVE ME A CALL.

RUBBER: Informal word for condom. Use ERASER.

SLEEPING PARTNER: Use SILENT PARTNER

SOLICITOR: Use ATTORNEY or LAWYER

TO WASH UP: In the U.S. this expression means to wash your face and/or hands. Use instead WASH THE DISHES.

TRAMP: Use HOBO or HOMELESS PERSON, a tramp can also mean a loose woman.

WHERE'S THE LADIES / GENTS?: Use, WHERE'S THE LADIES' / MEN'S ROOM? Or WHERE'S THE REST ROOM?

## WORDS AND TERMS TO BE AVOIDED BY AN AMERICAN IN BRITAIN

VEST, SUSPENDERS and PANTS:  Instead, use WAISTCOAT, BRACES and TROUSERS respectively.

KNICKERS:  This term means panties in U.K.  Use KNICKERBOCKERS.

I'M POOPED:  Use instead I'M EXHAUSTED.

I'M STUFFED:  Possibly vulgar, use I'M FULL.

BUGGER:  An offensive word in British English.

BUMMER:  Use instead NUISANCE or DISAPPOINTING.

BUM STEER:  Use instead BAD ADVICE or BAD DIRECTIONS.

FANNY:  Vulgar, use BOTTOM or BEHIND.

FANNY PACK:  Possibly vulgar, use BUM BAG.

GET A BANG OUT OF SOMEONE:  Possibly vulgar, use GET A KICK OUT OF SOMEONE

TRAMP:  Only use this if you mean a hobo.  It does not mean a loose woman in the U.K.

SCHOOL:  This is not used for university or higher education in the U.K.

SHAGGING FLIES:  This might not only sound obscene, but impossible.  Try RETREIVING AND RETURNING BASEBALLS

WASH UP:  This means to wash the dishes in Britain.  Try WASH YOUR HANDS instead.

**SOME WORDS WHICH HAVE DIFFERENT MEANINGS**

The following American words have quite different meanings in the U.K.

JUMPER, KNICKERS, SUSPENDERS, VEST and PUMPS are listed under CLOTHING DIFFERENCES found on page 33

DRESSER, VALANCE, BUREAU, COT, DAVENPORT, and HASSOCK are listed under DIFFERENT FURNISHING TERMS found on page 138

The following words are in are in the U.S.-U.K. Lexicons

DEADHEAD, DRY GOODS, GREEN CARD, HOMELY, JUG, LOFT, NERVY, CORDIAL, LEERY, SLATE, TABLE, SHINGLE, CRUET, PROCTOR, FAG, CRANKY, REDCAP, S.T.D., TWISTER, YARD, LEAN-TO, WASH UP, MARQUEE, and PAVEMENT

# IDIOMS AND EXPRESSIONS

Here is a list comparing British expressions with similar expressions used in the U.S.

*The abbreviations s/o and s/t stand for someone and something respectively*

| U.K. Term | U.S. Equivalent |
| --- | --- |
| A dab hand at s/t | A crackerjack at s/t |
| A storm in a teacup | Tempest in a teapot |
| At the end of one's tether | At the end of one's rope |
| Bang on | Right on |
| Beat them hollow | Clean their clocks |
| Belt up! | Shut up! |
| Blot one's copybook | Hurt one's reputation |
| Bob's your uncle | And there you have it |
| Bright spark | Smart cookie |
| Browned off | Teed off |
| Bunk off | Play hookey |
| Chat up | Come on to |
| Cheesed off | Teed off |
| Clapped out | Worn out |
| Come a cropper | Fall down |
| Common or garden | Garden variety |
| Daylight robbery | Highway robbery |
| Different as chalk and cheese | Comparing two very different people |
| Do a moonlight flit | Sneak out in the night |
| Do the dirty on s/o | Give s/o the shaft |
| Drop a clanger | Make a big faux pas |
| Dull as ditchwater | Dull as dishwater |
| Feel peckish | Have the munchies |

| U.K. Term | U.S. Equivalent |
| --- | --- |
| Full marks for… | Deserves an A for… |
| Get the wind up | All shook up |
| Get your knickers in a twist | Have a hissy fit |
| Give it a miss | Skip it / Pass it up + |
| Give s/o their cards | Give s/o a pink slip |
| Go spare | Go berserk + |
| Happy as a sandboy | Happy as a clam |
| Hard cheese! | Tough! |
| Have a lie-in | To sleep in |
| Have a natter | Shoot the breeze |
| Heath Robinson device | Rube Goldberg device |
| Hell for leather | Hell bent for leather |
| Home and dry | Home free |
| How's tricks | How's it going + |
| If the cap fits | If the shoe fits |
| In a trice | In a heartbeat./ New York minute |
| In donkey's years | In forever |
| In future | In the future |
| In Queer Street | Up the creek + |
| In someone's good books | In someone's good graces + |
| Keep your pecker up | Keep your chin up + |
| Knock on effect | Domino effect + |
| Knock spots off | Knock the socks off |
| Knocked for six | Thrown for a loop |
| Land s/o with | Saddle s/o with |
| Left holding the baby | Left holding the bag |
| Look at s/o old fashioned | Give s/o a disapproving look |
| Look like death warmed up | Look like death warmed over |
| Lumber s/o with | Stick s/o with |
| Make heavy weather of s/t | Make a big deal out of s/t |

| U.K. Term | U.S. Equivalent |
|---|---|
| Mug up on | Bone up on |
| Not on your nelly! | No way! |
| Off the beaten track | Off the beaten path |
| Off one's trolley | Off one's rocker + |
| On my tod | On my lonesome |
| On tenterhooks | On pins and needles |
| On the dole | On unemployment |
| On the never never | On installments |
| Out on the tiles | Out having a wild time |
| Over the moon | Ecstatic |
| Pack it in! | Stop it! |
| Packed up | Went kaput |
| Panic stations | Pandemonium + |
| Past praying for | Beyond hope |
| Peg out | Kick the bucket |
| Play gooseberry | Chaperone s/o |
| Potter around | Putter around |
| Pull your socks up | Try harder |
| Put it on the slate | Put it on the tab |
| Rolls Royce of…. | Cadillac of… |
| Rough diamond | Diamond in the rough |
| Round the bend | Up the wall + |
| Run with the hare and hunt with the hounds | Play both ends against the middle + |
| Save one's bacon | Save one's skin |
| Send s/o to Coventry | Give s/o the silent treatment |
| Skeleton in the cupboard | Skeleton in the closet |
| Slap up | Bang up |
| Slow coach | Slow poke |
| Spend a penny | Use the bathroom |

| U.K. Term | U.S. Equivalent |
|---|---|
| Spot on | On the money / On the nose |
| Stand for office | Run for office |
| Stone the crows! | Holy cow! |
| Stop on a sixpence | Stop on a dime |
| Sure as eggs are eggs | Sure as shootin' |
| Suss it out | Scope it out |
| Take a recce | Check it out + |
| Take the biscuit | Take the cake + |
| Take the mickey out of s/o | Razz s/o |
| Talk the hind legs off a donkey | Talk up a storm |
| Tart up | Gussy up |
| Ten a penny | A dime a dozen |
| The book of words | The instruction book |
| The penny dropped | The light came on |
| Thin as a rake | Skinny as a rail |
| Throw a spanner in the works | Throw a monkey wrench in the works |
| Tinker's cuss | Tinker's damn |
| Too big for his boots | Too big for his britches |
| Up my street | Up my alley |
| Went like a bomb | Took off + |
| When it comes to the crunch | When push comes to shove + |
| With knobs on | In spades |
| Wouldn't touch it with a barge pole | Wouldn't touch it with a ten foot pole |
| Yell blue murder | Yell bloody murder |
| You're having me on! | You're putting me on! |

Here is a list comparing American expressions with similar expressions used in the U.K.

| U.S. Term | U.K. Equivalent |
| --- | --- |
| A crackerjack at s/t | A dab hand at s/t |
| A day late and a dollar short, to be | Miss out on s/t |
| A dime a dozen | Ten a penny |
| A shoo-in | Certain to win / be appointed |
| All shook up | Get the wind up |
| All tied up (in sports) | Tied + |
| Any more you don't... | These days you don't... |
| At the end of one's rope | At the end of one's tether |
| Bang up | Slap up |
| Bar hopping | Going on a pub crawl |
| Beat up on | Beat up + |
| Beat up on oneself | Punish oneself |
| Behind the eight ball | Without options / Snookered (see Snookered U.S.) |
| Big time | In a big way / And how! |
| Blow off s/o | Dismiss / Ignore s/o |
| Bone up on | Mug up on |
| Break up housekeeping, to | To split up / Divorce |
| Bring s/o up to speed (hip) | Bring s/o up to date |
| Broke me up | Cracked me up + |
| Buffaloed | Confused for gain |
| Bug out | Scarper / Sneak out |
| Bum rap, a | A raw deal |
| Bum steer, a | Bad advice / Bad directions |
| Bummed me out | Upset me + |
| Burned me up | Browned me off |
| Butt out! | Stop butting in ! |
| Cadillac of.... | Rolls Royce of.... |
| Catch some Z's [zeez] | Have a zizz |
| Chill out! (hip slang) | Calm down! + |

| U.S. Term | U.K. Equivalent |
|---|---|
| Clean their clocks | Beat them hollow |
| Close call + | Close shave + |
| Close the barn door after the horse is out | Close the stable door after the horse has bolted |
| Come on to | Chat up |
| Come unglued | Go crazy + |
| Compare apples and oranges | Compare two different things |
| Compare apples with apples | Compare things in a similar category |
| Cool one's jets | Dampen one's ardour |
| Cotton pickin' hands | Filthy hands |
| Cotton to s/o | Take a liking to s/o |
| Cotton up to | Suck up to + |
| Crack a window | Open a window a crack |
| Crazy as a loon | Have bats in the belfry / Batty |
| Cry uncle | Admit defeat |
| Cut loose | Go wild |
| Cut up | Act the fool / Muck about |
| Diamond in the rough, a | A rough diamond |
| Do a double take | Take a closer look |
| Do a number on | Hurt / Damage |
| Do a snow job | Attempt to deceive or persuade through flattery or exaggeration |
| Do over | Do up |
| Dog and pony show | Farcical happening |
| Doggone | Darn + |
| Domino effect + | Knock on effect |
| Don't mind then! | Never mind then! + |
| Down the pike | Down the line + |
| Duke it out | Fight it out + |
| Dull as dishwater | Dull as ditchwater |
| Every which way | In all directions + |
| Exact same | Very same |

| U.S. Term | U.K. Equivalent |
|---|---|
| Feel punk | Feel unwell + |
| Fill out a form + | Fill in a form |
| Flip 'em the bird (hip slang) | Make a V sign |
| Fresh out of | Just ran out of |
| From the get go | From the word go + |
| Garden variety | Common or garden |
| Get a charge / bang out of | Get a kick out of + |
| Get the best of | Get the better of + |
| Gets old | Gets tedious/dull + |
| Give me some sugar | Give me a kiss |
| Give s/o a licking | Give s/o a hiding |
| Give s/o a pink slip | Give s/o their cards |
| Give s/o the bum's rush | Abruptly dismiss s/o |
| Give s/o the finger + | Make a V sign |
| Give s/o the shaft | Do the dirty on s/o |
| Give s/o the silent treatment | Send s/o to Coventry |
| Go Dutch treat | Go Dutch |
| Go figure | Try and figure that one out |
| Goof off | Skive off |
| Grandfathered in | Permitted because of pre-existing conditions |
| Graveyard shift | Night shift |
| Grossed me out (hip slang) | Disgusted me + |
| Gussy up | Tart up |
| Hang a right (or left) | Turn right |
| Happy as a clam | Happy as a sandboy |
| Haul ass (vulgar) | Move along |
| Have a hissy fit | Get your knickers in a twist |
| Have **at** it! | Go to it! |
| Have the munchies | Feel peckish |
| Held for ransom | Held to ransom |
| Hell bent for leather | Hell for leather |

| U.S. Term | U.K. Equivalent |
|-----------|-----------------|
| Hem and Haw | Hum and Ha |
| Hightail it | Go at top speed |
| Highway robbery | Daylight robbery |
| Hit the sack | Hit the hay + |
| Hogtied | Restrained / Thwarted |
| Holy cow! | Stone the crows! |
| Home free | Home and dry |
| If the shoe fits | If the cap fits |
| In a (blue) funk | Feeling down + |
| In a heartbeat./ New York minute | In a trice / In two ticks |
| In back | In the back + |
| In back of | Behind + |
| In forever | In donkey's years |
| In the loop (hip) | In the know |
| Katty corner from | Diagonally across from |
| Kick butt (hip slang) | Stir people up |
| Knock yourself out! | Go for your life |
| Knock the socks off | Knock spots off |
| Left holding the bag | Left holding the baby |
| Let go | Made redundant |
| Lie like a rug, to | To lie through one's teeth + |
| Look like death warmed over | Look like death warmed up |
| Low rent | Low class |
| Luck out | Be very lucky / Be in luck + |
| Make out (with s/o) | Snog / Get off with s/o |
| Make out like a bandit | To get a bargain / Be very successful |
| Make over - n. | Face lift + |
| Make over - v. | Do up |
| Mexican standoff | Stalemate |
| Money for jam + | Money for old rope |
| Nip and tuck | Touch and go + |

| U.S. Term | U.K. Equivalent |
|---|---|
| Off the beaten path | Off the beaten track |
| Off the rack (clothing) | Off the peg |
| On my lonesome | By myself / On my tod |
| On pins and needles | On tenterhooks |
| On the fritz | On the blink + |
| On the lam | On the run + |
| On the money | Spot on |
| On the nose | Spot on |
| On the rag (crude slang) | Irritable / Grumpy |
| On the wrong side of the tracks | In the wrong part of town |
| Party animal | Party goer / Raver |
| Party pooper | s/o who spoils a party |
| Philadelphia lawyer | Genius + |
| Play both ends against the middle + | Run with the hare and hunt with the hounds |
| Play hookey | Bunk off |
| Play phone tag | To call one another's answering machine without speaking in person |
| Pooped | Knackered |
| Put it on the tab + | Put it on the slate |
| Put the moves on | Chat up |
| Putter around | Potter around |
| Railroad s/o | Press-gang s/o / Convict hastily and unjustly |
| Rattled my cage | Wound me up |
| Razz s/o | Take the mickey out of s/o |
| Ride shotgun, to | To ride in the passenger seat |
| Right on | Spot on / Bang on |
| Rube Goldberg device | Heath Robinson device |
| Run for office | Stand for office |
| Run that by me again? | Would you repeat that? |
| Same difference | Same thing + |

| U.S. Term | U.K. Equivalent |
| --- | --- |
| Scarf down | Scoff down |
| Scope it out | Take a recce / Suss it out |
| Set up housekeeping | Set up / Move in together + |
| Shine up to | Suck up to |
| Shoot hoops | Play basketball |
| Shoot the breeze | Have a natter |
| Shoot! | Damn! + |
| Skeleton in the closet | Skeleton in the cupboard |
| Skinny as a rail | Thin as a rake |
| Skip it / Pass it up + | Give it a miss |
| Sleep over, to | Spend the night (children's term) |
| Slip s/o a mickey | Slip a narcotic in a drink |
| Slow poke | Slow coach |
| Smart cookie | Bright spark |
| Snookered (rhymes with cooker) | Conned + (see Behind the eight ball U.S.) |
| Son of a gun! | Well I never! |
| Sounds like Greek to me + | It's all double Dutch to me |
| Stand on / in line | Stand in a queue |
| Stick s/o with | Lumber / Land s/o with |
| Stop on a dime | Stop on a sixpence |
| Sure as shootin' | Sure as eggs |
| Take the cake + | Take the biscuit |
| Talk up a storm | Talk the hind legs off a donkey |
| Teed off | Browned off / Cheesed off |
| Tempest in a teapot | A storm in a teacup |
| The light came on | The penny dropped |
| The whole ball of wax | The whole (kit and) caboodle + |
| The whole nine yards | The whole (kit and) caboodle + |
| Throw a monkey wrench in the works | Throw a spanner in the works |
| Thrown for a loop | Knocked sideways / Knocked for six |

| U.S. Term | U.K. Equivalent |
|---|---|
| To go (at a fast food restaurant) | To take away |
| Too big for his britches | Too big for his boots |
| Took off + | Went like a bomb |
| Tough! | Hard cheese! |
| Up and at 'em | Up and at it |
| Up my alley | Up my street |
| Up the creek + | In Queer Street |
| Wait on line | Stand in a queue |
| Want out | Want to get out |
| Water over the dam | Water under the bridge + |
| Way to go! | Good going! |
| Way too… | Much too… |
| We're history (hip) | Let's get going + |
| Went kaput | Packed up |
| What a bummer | What a nuisance + |
| What a stitch! | What a hoot! + |
| When push comes to shove + | When it comes to the crunch |
| Whipped | Knackered |
| Wouldn't touch it with a ten foot pole | Wouldn't touch it with a barge pole |
| Yea high | So high + |
| Yell bloody murder | Yell blue murder |
| You're putting me on! | You're having me on! |

To *put one's best foot forward* means to do one's best in the U.S. In Britain it means to walk briskly. To *cotton on to* someone means to take a liking to someone in the U.S. In British English to *cotton on* means to catch on to an idea. To be *in a funk* has quite a different meaning in the U.K. It means to be in a state of panic. In the U.S. it means to be depressed. To *feel one's oats* means to feel lively in British English, but in American English it means to feel self-important.

## COMMON METAPHORICAL BASEBALL TERMS

Americans often use sport terms in conversations. One sport from which a lot of terms are borrowed is Baseball, which, by the way, evolved from the British game "Rounders".

| U.S. Term | U.K. Equivalent |
| --- | --- |
| A ball park figure | A rough estimate |
| A tough call | A difficult decision |
| Batting a thousand | Going great guns |
| Batting zero | Getting nowhere |
| Cover all bases | Take care of everything |
| Didn't get to first base | Didn't accomplish anything |
| Get to home base | Achieve one's goal |
| Make a home run | Succeed |
| Out in left field | Off track |
| Strike out | Fail |
| Switch hitter | Bisexual person |
| The bases are loaded | It's a make or break situation |
| Throw s/o a curve (ball) | Give s/o a problem |
| To be off base | To hold a mistaken idea |
| Touch base | Get in touch with s/o |
| Whole new ball game | Starting from scratch |
| You're up / You're at bat | It's up to you / It's your turn |

Playing *pepper* means warming up by catching and returning balls. Practising catching balls in the out field is known as *shagging flies*.

## SOME OLDER BRITISH WORDS AND EXPRESSIONS YOU MAY HEAR

| U.K. Term | U.S. Equivalent |
| --- | --- |
| Bath chair | Wheelchair |
| Bathing drawers | Bathing suit |
| Bounder | Scoundrel |

| U.K. Term | U.S. Equivalent |
|---|---|
| Carriage rug | Lap robe |
| Char / charwoman | Cleaning lady |
| Charabanc | Tour bus |
| Geyser | Instant hot water heater |
| Ironmonger | Hardware store |
| Outside (on a bus) | Upstairs |
| Ripping | Terrific |
| Rum | Odd / Strange |
| Shape | JELLO |
| Wireless | Radio |
| Wood wool | Excelsior |

## SOME OLDER U.S. WORDS AND EXPRESSIONS YOU MAY HEAR

| U.S. Term | U.K. Equivalent |
|---|---|
| A five spot / fin | A five dollar bill |
| Aforenoon | Morning |
| Apple polisher | One who curries favour with another |
| Barn burner | An exciting event |
| Blues harp | Mouth organ |
| Bodacious | Remarkable / Outstanding |
| Broad / Gal / Dame | Chick / Bird |
| Bumbershoot | Brolly |
| C- Note / a C | One hundred dollar bill |
| Cheaters | Reading glasses |
| Chew the fat / rag | Have a natter |
| Church key | A beverage can or bottle opener |
| Colored glasses | Sun glasses |

| U.S. Term | U.K. Equivalent |
| --- | --- |
| Comfort station | Public convenience |
| Copacetic | A-OK + |
| Cowpoke | Cowboy |
| Cut a rug, to | Dance |
| Dime store / 5&10 | Low cost general store |
| Dimestore glasses | Reading glasses purchased without a prescription |
| Directional | Indicator |
| Dressing (with poultry) | Stuffing |
| Druggist | Pharmacist |
| Excelsior (former brand name) | Wood wool |
| Fire plug | Fire hydrant |
| Fly window (car) | Quarter light |
| For lands sake | Oh my giddy aunt |
| Gandy dancer | Platelayer (railway) |
| Gobs of | Bags of |
| Goose egg (to score zero) | Duck / Duck's egg |
| Have one's druthers | Have one's way |
| High test (gas) | High octane |
| Hoofer | Professional dancer |
| Hop | Dance party |
| Icebox | Refrigerator |
| In a coon's age | In donkey's years |
| In the back forty (humorous) | At the bottom of the garden |
| Lap robe | Rug (light blanket) |
| Lickety-split | Hell for leather |
| Light bill | Electricity bill |
| Milquetoast | Wimp |
| Monkeyshines | Shenanigans |
| Normal school | Teachers training college |
| Oleo | Margarine |

| U.S. Term | U.K. Equivalent |
|---|---|
| Phonograph | Gramophone |
| Phosphate | Soft drink |
| Pill | A disagreeable person |
| Pocket book | Purse / Handbag |
| Puff | Eiderdown |
| Put on the dog | Put on side |
| Quinine water | Indian tonic water |
| Ride herd | Supervise / Boss |
| Ride Shank's mare | Take Shanks's pony |
| Sawbuck | A ten dollar bill |
| Seltzer bottle | Soda siphon |
| Shag | Dance |
| Soda jerk | S/o who works at a soda fountain |
| Spider (regional Midwest) | Frying pan |
| Steamer rug | Rug |
| Strike pay dirt | On the scent |
| Swell | Dandy |
| Tradelast / T.L. | Response to a compliment |
| Two bits | Twenty-five cents (25¢) |
| Victrola | Wind-up gramophone |
| Visiting fireman | Special visitor in town |
| Warm over (food) | Warm up |
| What the Sam Hill! | What the hell! |
| While sawing logs | While sleeping |
| White gas | Unleaded petrol |
| Wing window (car) | Quarter light |
| Wood alcohol | Methyl alcohol |

The words Pocket book (meaning a hand bag) and Druggist are still commonly used by older Americans, who also may pronounce measure and pleasure, mayzhure and playzhure. Rations may be pronounced rayshns, and long-lived may sometimes be pronounced long līved.

## INTERESTING AMERICAN EXPRESSIONS

FOR THE LONGEST TIME in place of FOR A LONG TIME.

I HAD THE HARDEST TIME in place of I HAD A HARD TIME.

ANY MORE is sometimes used at the beginning or end of a sentence and approximates the meaning of THESE DAYS or NOWADAYS. e.g. "Any more you can't buy red gloves."

## SOME DIFFERENT PREPOSITIONS

| *U.S. Term* | *U.K. Term* |
|---|---|
| Cut off (in traffic) | Cut up |
| Do over (Make over) | Do up |
| Hold up / Wait up | Hold on + |
| In heat | On heat |
| In tow | On tow |
| Sell out (property) | Sell up |
| Top off | Top up |
| Wait on (tables) | Wait at |
| Wait on | Wait for + |

The preposition *of* is used more readily in the U.S. e.g. *all of my life, ouside of the U.S.* The prepositions *out* and *up* are never used in the U.S. with the terms, *packed out* and *phone up.*

## SOME DIFFERENT SUFFIXES

| U.S. Term | U.K. Term |
|---|---|
| Dance class | Dancing class |
| Driver's license | Driving licence |
| Headed for | Heading for + |
| Race car | Racing car |
| Race meet | Race meeting |
| Rowboat | Rowing boat |
| Sailboat | Sailing boat |
| Sawed-off | Sawn-off |
| Scrub brush | Scrubbing brush |

*"Jim really knocked spots off Bo last night"*

(see page 149)

# *EXPLANATIONS*

## TERM CLARIFICATIONS

**Appraise:** In the U.S. a house is *appraised* by an *appraiser*. In the U.K. it is *valued* by a *valuer*. Conversely job performance is usually evaluated in the U.S. rather than *appraised* as it is in Britain.

**Bikini:** A bikini in the U.S. can mean a man's brief swim suit or a woman's two piece swim suit. In the U.K. it only is used in referring to a woman's two piece swim suit.

**Blow out:** A blow out has several meanings in the U.S. It can mean a tyre suddenly losing air. It can also mean a big party. A blow out sale means a big sale with great price reductions.

**Bollard:** A common word in British English. It can either be used for a traffic diverter, or for a short upright metal post to secure a ship at a wharf. This word is only known in the U.S. by nautical folk, for the latter meaning. It is unknown by the average American.

**Broil/Grill:** In the U.S. broiling implies cooking something directly under the flame, while grilling implies cooking something over the flame. The term grill in the U.S. may also mean frying something on a large, solid metal plate which is called a grill. In British English the word grill covers both the American words broil and grill. There is also another American term which implies that the food has first been boiled, then roasted, broiled or grilled. The term is *broasted*.

**Bungalow:** In British English a bungalow is any one story house. A bungalow in the U.S. indicates a small simple one story house, often of a particular design.

**Café:** A café in American English can also have the additional meaning of a night-club, as well as a coffee shop.

**Call:** If an American says, *"They're calling for rain"*; he means that the forecast is indicating rain is likely. If a thermostat is set high enough for the heat to come on; the thermostat is said to be *calling for heat*.

**Can:** In the U.K. one *bottles* fruit in a KILNER jar, in the U.S. one *cans* fruit in a MASON jar.

**Chemist:** In the U.K. a chemist can refer to a laboratory chemist, a pharmacy or a pharmacist.

**Cider:** In the U.K. cider is an alcoholic beverage. In the U.S. cider is usually unfermented apple juice but *hard* cider is alcoholic.

**Condominium/Condo:** (From the Latin words *com* and *dominium*) A common word in the U.S. for a complex of individually owned houses or apartments whose owners belong to a legal association for the proper and continued maintenance of all commonly owned property on which their residences are located. The term refers either to the entire complex or to a single unit in the complex. Owners often time-share or lease their "Condos" to others.

**Cool:** Americans use cool in a variety of ways. It can mean modern, liberal, up-to-date (she's cool, that's cool); acceptable, not a threat, in-the-know (he's cool); an exclamation of approval, appreciation or delight (cool!)

**Crack:** If an American asks you to crack a window, he wants you to open it slightly.

**Crazy:** The British term crazy paving is as perplexing to most Americans as the term crazy quilt is to most Britons. In both cases the term crazy means *patchwork*.

**Cross ventilation:** In the U.S., a room is said to have good cross ventilation if it has windows at opposite ends, permitting a good movement of air through the room.

**Drapes:** Drapes and draperies are both used for curtains in the U.S. Draperies is considered the preferred word by some people, but drapes is still the more common word. The term *window treatments* covers all the material at a window. Curtains in the U.S. usually do not draw.

**Drug store/Pharmacy:** While these terms are often used interchangeably in the U.S., there is a distinction to be made. A pharmacy is a section in a large department store, while a drug store is a separate or privately owned shop.

**Dumb waiter:** A dumb waiter in both Britain and America is a device for transporting food between floors; however in Britain it has an additional meaning of a revolving food holder at a dining table. This is known as a lazy susan in the U.S.

**Duplex:** A duplex (also known as a *two family*), refers to two semi-detached single houses on one lot. The houses are often separated in the middle by two garages These are often used as rental property. In some areas a duplex may refer to two rental properties one above the other.

**Guy:** If used in the plural it refers to men *and* women in the U.S.

**Hire/Rent:** The terms *hire* and *rent* are often used interchangeably in Britain. However, in the U.S. *hire* refers to people, while *rent* usually refers to things, such as a video tape or car . *Lease* implies a long term legal obligation in the renting of items. The term *let* has pretty much fallen from popular use in the U.S. Normally the term *rent out* is used instead of the term *let*, although *rent* alone is often used. The distinctions in meaning are easily understood in context.

**Holiday:** A holiday in the U.S. usually means a bank holiday, (known as a legal holiday). *The holidays*, can refer to a bank holiday weekend, or it can refer to the period between Thanksgiving, which occurs at the end of November, and New Year's day. *Vacation* is the usual equivalent of the British word *holiday*.

**Hospital:** In Britain, if one is admitted, one goes *to hospital*. If one is visiting, one goes to *the hospital*. In the US, there is no distinction. It is always *the* hospital.

**Icing and Frosting:** Are often used interchangeably in the U.S., though more accurately icing refers to a smooth topping and frosting to a whipped or creamy topping. Frosting is not used in Britain.

**John:** The word *john*, in the U.S., has several meanings. The *john* means the toilet (originally a term used for an outdoor toilet for men, the women's being the *Jane*). A *john* means a hooker's (prostitute's) trick. A *dear john letter* means a good-bye letter.

**Jug:** A jug in British English would be known as a *pitcher* in American English. A jug in America is a large vessel with a handle and a narrow neck, usually with a stopper.

**Mall and Plaza:** In the U.S. a *plaza* [plahza] is a shopping center with a collection of individual shops and stores sharing parking facilities. Whereas, a *mall* [mawl] is a collection of individual shops and stores constructed under one roof with a common indoor, air conditioned promenade. It is usually much larger than a plaza, and contains a mixture of large department stores and smaller shops and restaurants.

**Mail:** In general, the word *mail* may be substituted in the U.S. for the British term *post*. However, there are some exceptions, such as, Post mark, Post Office, and the Postal Service.

**Mains:** Water and electricity are shut off at the *main* in the U.S., but at the *mains* in Britain. The terms *mains pressure* (for water), and *run off the mains* (for electricity) have no good equivalent in the U.S.

**Marquee:** The word marquee, according to Webster's dictionary came about from a false attempt at making a singular word from marquise around 1680. Marquee was originally used for a shelter for a marquis or marquise. The word came to mean a large outdoor tent in British English, and an awning projecting over an entrance in American English. Younger Americans tend to use the word mostly to describe an illuminated sign either over a theatre or by the road.

**Medicare / Medicaid:** Medicare is a U.S. government program of medical insurance for retirees and disabled people. Medicaid is a federal and State program for indigents.

**Knock up:** The word knock up can be used in a variety of ways in British English. One can knock up at tennis (warm up). One can knock up a meal in a hurry, and one can even knock oneself up (out). The only meaning of *knock up* in American English is a slang expression meaning *to make a girl pregnant*.

**Pocketbook:** This word is used by older Americans to mean a handbag. To younger Americans the term is usually applied to financial resources e.g. "That white sport's car is too much for my pocketbook."

**Porch:** A porch in England is a small sheltered area outside a building. In the U.S. a porch can also mean a much larger often elevated area at the front or back of the house where one can sit. This would be called a verandah in Britain.

**Realtor:** Realtor is trademark. It refers to a real estate agent who is a member of the National Association of Real Estate Boards. It is commonly used by Americans for any real estate agent.

**Redneck:** This term often refers to an intractable person with set ideas and opinions. It may also connote a lack of education and / or intelligence, but not necessarily. The word itself comes from white laborers in the south who had sunburned necks from bending over in the fields.

**Rug:** In the U.K. a rug can be used to describe a light blanket used to cover oneself, or to sit on at a picnic. This is known in the U.S. as a *throw*. A large carpet may be referred to as a rug in the U.S. A slang term for a hairpiece in the U.S. is a rug.

**Sale:** In the U.S., the word sale is used in many ways:

| | |
|---|---|
| Blowout sale | a clearance sale |
| Garage sale | a family selling used items from their garage |
| Tag sale | a jumble sale |
| Trunk sale | sale of last season's merchandise in a clothing store |
| Yard Sale | same as garage sale |

**Shingle:** A shingle in the U.S. means either an asphalt or wooden tile, or a small sign outside a business. Quite different from the British meaning of beach pebbles.

**Tap:** A tap in the house is known as a *faucet* in the U.S. An outdoor tap or a stopcock is called a *spigot*. However water from the faucet is called tap water.

**Toboggan:** A toboggan in the U.S. is a sled without runners, which curves up at the front. A sled is the U.S. term for the British word toboggan.

**Vet:** The word vet in the U.S. can either mean a veterinarian or a war veteran. In Britain it is an abbreviation for veterinary surgeon.

**Visit with:** In the U.S. this can either mean visit in the British sense (to go and socialize with) or it can be used in place of to *chat with*. This is a rather informal expression.

**Warden**: In British English the term warden refers to the governor of a hospital, college, or a YMCA. A prison governor is called a warden in American English.

**Whistle stop:** A whistle stop is a small town along a railway line in the U.S. It can also mean a short appearance by a performing group, or a politician in such a town.

**Yard:** The word yard in America refers to the area around a house and roughly equates to the British word garden. The word garden in the U.S. is used in reference to a cultivated area, such as a rose garden or a vegetable garden. A yard in British English is a paved area.

# NOTES ON SYMBOLS

## THE R$_X$ SYMBOL

This symbol **R$_x$** is seen a lot in the U.S. On a medical prescription it is probably an abbreviation for the Latin word *recipere*, meaning "to take". There is another theory though, that the symbol represents Jupiter, the god of the sky and the rain. This symbol, which stands for prescription is often seen outside a pharmacy. It is often used in everyday print, e.g. 'Do you have heartburn? R$_x$ a short walk after meals.' It is also sometimes used as a symbol to identify a pharmacy.

## THE DOLLAR ($) SYMBOL

Some have suggested that the dollar symbol $, was created by superimposing a "U" over an "S," with the bottom of the "U" cut off. An interesting idea, but it has no validity. The true story is as follows.

In 1782 Thomas Jefferson made the Spanish coin, the *Eight Piece Reál* the official unit of currency, rather than the Pound. This coin was known by various names at the time by the English speaking community. It was most commonly called :

- The Spanish Dollar
- The Pillar Dollar
- The Silver Dollar
- Pieces of Eight.

The word "Dollar" at that time was used for various coins that were modeled on an ancient Bohemian Coin, the *Joachimsthaler*, named after the silver mine at Joachimstal (now Jachymov). This town, which is now in the Czech Republic, first minted coins in 1519. The name *Pillar*

*Dollar* came from the two pillars (representing the Pillars of Hercules at Gibraltar), which were engraved on the front of the *Eight Piece Reál* and two vertical lines came to be used as a shorthand for dollars. The "S" was placed over it to indicate plural. This coin, which was in common use throughout the Americas, was frequently cut into 8 pie shaped pieces for change; hence the name *pieces of eight*. To this day stock market prices are quoted in eighths of a dollar and the quarter, the 25 cent coin is known as two bits. The first U.S. dollar was minted in 1794 and was known as the *flowing hair* dollar.

## THE (£) SYMBOL

The Pound or Pound Sterling is represented by the symbol £. It is an elaboration of an L for Libra, which is Latin for pound weight. Historically, the terms *pound* and *pound sterling* originated in Britain during the 8th century. At that time a sterling was the basic monetary unit, and 240 sterlings which weighed a pound was known as a pound of sterling, and later a pound. The pound was initially convertible into silver and later into gold. The gold standard was abandoned in 1931

## THE (#) SYMBOL

In the U.S. the symbol # before a number means number, rather like No., which is used in both countries. If placed after a number, it means pounds weight, e.g. #3 means number 3, whereas 3# means 3 lbs. (lbs is also used in both countries.) This symbol is rarely used in Britain. It is usually called the pound sign in the U.S. and hash in the U.K. Many years ago it was known as the tic tac toe sign or the number sign in the U.S. The British terms for this symbol; hash, gate and square, are unknown in the U.S. The American term pound sign can cause confusion between this symbol and the £ symbol.

## PLC.

PLC. is an abbreviation meaning Public Limited Company in the U.K., and is often seen at the end of a company's name. Ltd. is also used. These abbreviations have a similar meaning to the letters Inc. often seen at the end of an American company's name. There is usually a comma preceding the letters Inc., but not with Plc or Ltd.

# ART TERMS

Art terms are mostly the same throughout the English speaking world, but here are some interesting terms you may come across in museums and art galleries:

| Term. | Explanation |
|---|---|
| Ajouré [azhouray] | Elaborately cut or perforated metalwork |
| Amorino [amoreenoh] | Chubby, naked winged boy |
| Amphora [amforə] | Ancient Greek jar with two handles on either side of a short neck |
| Applied art | Art that is functional |
| Barbican | A fortified structure designed to protect an entrance |
| Barbotine [barbo·teen] | The decoration of pottery in relief using semi-liquid clay |
| Baroque [*Am* barŏk] [*Br* barŏk] | Very ornate artwork and architecture and music from the 17th and 18th centuries |
| Bozzetto | A first stage sketch toward making a tapestry or fresco |
| Bright cut | A type of decorative engraving done on silver to produce a glitter effect |
| Cabriole leg [cabreeōl] | A leg on furniture resembling a goat's leg |
| Caisson [kayson] | A sunken panel in a coffered ceiling |
| Capital | The ornamental stonework at the top of a column |

| Term. | Explanation |
|-------|-------------|
| Cartoon | A full size archetype of a tapestry or fresco. This is the last of a three stage process (see bozzetto and modello) |
| Casino | An ornamental pavilion or small house on the grounds of a larger house |
| Cob | A building material consisting of clay, straw sand and sometimes gravel |
| Craquelure [crakəlure] | A pattern of fine cracks found on old paintings that can be used to determine its authenticity |
| Criselling [crizeling] | Fine cracks on the surface of old glass |
| Crown glass | Hand blown glass used for windows |
| Deckle edge | A ragged edge found on hand made paper |
| Dhurrie [dûree] | A type of tapestry or rug |
| Entrelacs [ontralacs] | An ornamental design on a flat surface |
| Entresol [ontrasol] | Mezzanine |
| Faience [fay·ence] | Tin glazed eathenware |
| Gauffering [gōfering] | An embossed pattern on textiles |
| Gothic | A style of architecture with pointed arches prevalent in the 12th - 16th centuries in Europe |
| Gouache [goo·ash] | A painting done with opaque watercolors |
| High renaissance | The period between 1495 and 1520 A.D. |

| Term. | Explanation |
|---|---|
| Ignudo [ig·noo·do] | A male nude |
| Kinetic art | Art that has some mechanical movement |
| Kitsch [kich] | Mass produced art imitating elite art |
| Label | A band or scroll bearing an inscription |
| Loggia [lōzha] | A gallery |
| Maquette [mak·et] | A small 3D sketch, used as a model for a sculpture |
| Modello | A small, full color detailed painting for the proposed tapestry or fresco |
| Moiré [mwaray] | A rippled effect (such as in satin) |
| Montage [montazh] | The process of sticking one material on top of another |
| Mullion | A wood or stone partition in a window |
| Narrative painting | A painting that tells a story |
| Naturalism | The depiction of everyday things |
| Ormolu [ormoloo] | Gilded bronze used on ornamental objects |
| Piqué work [peekay] | Ivory or tortoiseshell dotted with specks of gold |
| Pop art | Art which depicts modern consumerism |
| Post modern | A modification of the Modernism style in the 20th century |
| Provenance | The record of all known previous owners and locations of a pice of art |

| **Term.** | **Explanation** |
|---|---|
| Putto (plural Putti) [pûtō / pûtee] | A plump naked boy, often a small stautue |
| Relief | A design projecting from a flat surface |
| Renaissance [*Am:* rena·sens] <br> [*Br:* re·**nay**·sens] | A revival period for the arts which began in the 14<sup>th</sup> century in Italy |
| Repoussé [rə·pŏ·say] | Metal beaten into a relief design from the back |
| Restoration style | Opulent English baroque style that started at the time of the restoration of Charles II to the throne |
| Rococo [rocōcō] | A late baroque style prevalent in the 18<sup>th</sup> century |
| Romanesque [raman·esk] | Pre-gothic art 8<sup>th</sup> - 12<sup>th</sup> centuries |
| Rotunda | A round building |
| Scagliola [scaglee·ohla] | Imitation marble |
| Striation [strī·āshn] | A pattern of narrow lines or srteaks |
| Trompe l'oeil [trŏmp lƏee] | Artwork, usually painted on a wall, that tricks the viewer into thinking he is seeing the actual objects |

*"Would it be O.K. if I wash up John?"* ... *"My dear chap, I wouldn't dream of letting you."* (see page 146)

The lexicographer Noah Webster is responsible for many of the spelling differences between Britain and America. His American Dictionary which came out in 1828 became the standard for U.S. spelling. Webster originally wanted Americans to use completely phonetic spelling, but later on he mellowed in his thinking.

# MISCELLANEOUS INFORMATION

I have found several differences between the countries that either don't fit into any particular category or are more of general interest than any practical use.

1. Americans will often say two times rather than twice. e.g. "We saw the show two times."

2. When spelling a word having two consecutive identical letters, like canned, most Britons will say "double n". Most Americans however will pronounce each letter separately.

3. The date on a form or a letter in Britain is expressed by putting the day, the month, then the year. In the U.S. the month comes first, followed by the day and then the year. The time is divided by a period in Britain, but a colon in the U.S.

4. A billion in the U.S. is 1000,000,000 or the equivalent of the British *milliard*. The British meaning of billion, which is a million million is slowly going out in favor of the American one thousand million.

5. Tarmac is used in the U.S. only when speaking of airport runways. Asphalt or black top is the term used for a road surface.

6. Telephones have numbers *and* letters on the dial in the U.S. The letters were dropped in Britain in the seventies. Many *800* and *888* numbers in the U.S. use letters as well as numbers.

7. To feel sick in British English means to feel nauseated. An American would say he felt sick to his stomach.

8. The American and British legal systems are somewhat different. A trial attorney, or counselor-at-law is the rough equivalent of a British barrister; but you can confer directly with a trial

attorney. In Britain you confer with your solicitor, who in turn confers with your barrister. Since 1970 the term *paralegal* has been used in the U.S. for someone trained to perform certain legal tasks for a lawyer. An articled clerk performs similar duties in Britain.

9. In both countries, some words are mainly written but seldom spoken. In the U.S. if you look through the yellow pages for a car rental agency, you will need to look under Automobile Rentals, though the term car is much more common than automobile. Similarly, a sign at the side of the road might read *Next Signal - Rose Street*; but in speaking, a person would say "next light." In Britain an equivalent is found in the WC sign. The average Briton does not ask where the WC is, though a foreign visitor might.

10. Most U.S. college courses start out with a course designation of 101 in the first year. The term 101 is often used in American speech to indicate a basic course, in a jocular sense. e.g. "He needs to take etiquette 101."

11. Some examples of words first used in America that have made their way back to Britain include: *lasso, moccasin, outlandish, widget, O.K.*.

12. Americans usually refer to *Paris, France* or *Rome, Italy*. This is because so many towns in the US have been named after European cities, e.g. *Athens, Georgia*, that there is a need to specify where the town or city is located.

13. Some nicknames of American men are not used in Britain, such as *Bud, Buzz, Chip, Chuck, Hank, Butch, Randy* and *Bubba* (regional South).

14. *Ate:* The pronunciation of *ate* is a little tricky. In America one should pronounce it *eight*. In Britain one is taught to pronounce it *et.*. This is confusing, but if you wish to have a command of

English wherever you are, it is necessary to change the way you pronounce *ate*.

15. The letters PTO for *please turn over* are often used when writing in Britain. Americans use the words *over* or *see over*, sometimes with an arrow. The letters N.B, from the Latin *nota bene* meaning *note well*, are often used in Britain, particularly in an instruction manual.

16. Some expressions that surprisingly, are used in both countries:
   - a piece of cake
   - not my cup of tea
   - in your neck of the woods
   - penny wise, pound foolish
   - the proof of the pudding...
   - mind your P's and Q's
   - it cost a pretty penny

*Many British English speaking people feel that American English is taking over as a form of global communication. I think that British English will be around for many years to come, but I cannot agree that one version of English is superior to the other.*